Contemporary's Whole Language Series

TEACHER'S GUIDE

Contemporary's Whole Language Series

TEACHER'S GUIDE

for

EXPRESSIONS and VIEWPOINTS

Volumes 1 and 2

CONTEMPORARY BOOKS

a division of NTC/CONTEMPORARY PUBLISHING GROUP
Lincolnwood, Illinois USA

Project Editors
Pat Fiene
Cathy Niemet

Writers
Karen Fox
Ted Knight

ISBN: 0-8092-3645-1

Published by Contemporary Books,
a division of NTC/Contemporary Publishing Group, Inc.,
4255 West Touhy Avenue,
Lincolnwood (Chicago), Illinois, 60712-1975 U.S.A.
Manufactured in the United States of America

3 4 5 6 7 8 9 0 QSR 12 11 10 9 8 7 6 5 4

CONTENTS

EXPRESSIONS 13

TO THE INSTRUCTOR

In 1992, Contemporary launched its groundbreaking whole-language program for adults—*Expressions* (short stories and poems), *Viewpoints* (nonfiction selections), and the *Teacher's Guide for Expressions and Viewpoints*.

The goal of the anthologies was to provide adult new readers and ESL readers with "real" fiction and nonfiction that happened to be written at low levels, rather than watered-down adaptations or formula pieces written to specifications. The goal of the teacher's guide was to incorporate the latest in reading pedagogy—the whole-language philosophy.

The popularity of the first two anthologies led Contemporary to develop two more parallel volumes in 1994—*Expressions: Volume 2* and *Viewpoints: Volume 2*. Featuring the same low reading levels as their predecessors, the second volumes provide students and instructors with over forty new selections that complement those found in *Expressions* and *Viewpoints*. Together, the four volumes in the program contain over eighty selections, giving students a wide range of topics and themes to choose from.

For your convenience, this expanded teacher's guide provides lesson plans for all four volumes under one cover. By popular demand, the overview of the whole-language philosophy that appeared in the 1992 edition of the guide has been retained and updated.

· ·

WHAT IS WHOLE LANGUAGE?

Whole language is difficult to define. It refers to a philosophy more than a method of teaching. Most of the theory and research pertaining to whole language has been based on its application with learners at the K through 8 levels, where the impact of this philosophy is most strongly felt. However, the principles on which whole language is based are easily adaptable to learners at all age levels.

An all-encompassing approach to learning and instruction, whole language is generally defined as a learner-centered approach in which language is the channel for teaching content. According to this philosophy, the development of spoken and written language skills centers around the experience, background, and needs of the learners. The whole-language philosophy recognizes that language and literacy development is most effectively achieved when reading, writing, speaking, listening, concept development, and thinking are interrelated. Therefore, strategies must acknowledge and exploit the interrelatedness of all these language components.

According to the whole-language philosophy, skills are not broken up into pieces and taught in isolation; they are related to meaningful contexts. On another level, whole language means that students are responsible for their own learning. Teachers become *facilitators* in the learning process in which they themselves become learners. As a result, the learning experience is dynamic and interactive.

The whole-language philosophy links topics and subject matter across the content areas. For example, issues covered in a "reading" context are examined for their connections to math, social studies, science, and other appropriate subject areas. This integration across content areas allows for a richer learning/teaching experience in which the learner is able to fully grasp the interrelatedness of knowledge.

. . . .

CHARACTERISTICS OF A WHOLE-LANGUAGE APPROACH

- **Language is kept whole.** Reading, writing, speaking, viewing, and listening are natural parts of each lesson.

- **Learner-centered.** Language lessons are geared to meet individual interests and needs. The curriculum is organized around broad themes within which each learner can explore his or her own interests.

- **Literature-based.** In order to come to literacy naturally, learners need exposure to high-impact reading material. This material is read to, by, and with learners in a variety of ways.

- **Context-rich.** Specific reading skills are taught within the context of rewarding material. This way, learners are introduced to the many forms of language and the rules guiding its use.

- **Writing-rich.** From the beginning, learners are encouraged to write. This helps establish links to language usage.

- **Talk-focused.** Because whole-language teachers know that learners need to talk to facilitate thinking, reading, and writing, they provide many opportunities for verbal interaction.

- **Activity-based.** Students learn best when they are actively involved in structuring their own learning. Learners should be permitted this flexibility. Classrooms must be designed to facilitate interaction.

- **Self-esteem building.** Learners in whole-language classrooms feel that they are capable. When a learner in a whole-language classroom does not seem to be functioning effectively, the facilitator should examine the program, the teaching, and the materials to better enable the student to learn.

- **Whole-class, small-group, and individual teaching/learning situations.** No single teaching methodology suits all students. Whole-language teachers use all of their knowledge and strategies with every class.

- **Fun!** The whole-language philosophy, though it involves hard work, is a marvelous way to teach.

(Adapted from the *Whole Language Umbrella Newsletter*, December 1986.)

· ·

WHOLE LANGUAGE AND THE ADULT LEARNER

How can whole-language principles enhance the learning experience for the adult learner? The whole-language approach is eminently suitable for adult learners from the ABE-level classroom to the GED level to transitional ESL for many reasons. Among them are:

- Adult learners bring a wealth of life experiences to the learning environment. Because it is learner-centered, the whole-language approach provides many opportunities to incorporate these experiences into the learning process.

- Adult learners are by nature more goal oriented than younger learners. Their learning is motivated by a strong sense of purpose. As a result, adult learners generally are more capable of taking responsibility for their own learning than are younger students.

- Adult learners often bring to the classroom setting their experiences working in small groups. Cooperative work teams and quality circles, for example, are a feature of many workplaces. The dynamics of the whole-language environment simulate this collaborative model. As a result, adult learners are able to transfer interactive strategies and procedures to their workplaces, families, and communities.

- Adults, by virtue of their prior experience and background, are more easily viewed by their instructors as equals in the learning experience, working with their facilitators toward shared goals.

· ·

HOW DOES CONTEMPORARY'S *WHOLE LANGUAGE SERIES* SATISFY THE PRINCIPLES OF WHOLE LANGUAGE?

- Questions and activities for each student book emphasize the interrelatedness of reading, writing, listening, speaking, and thinking. "Reflect" and "Write" sections feature questions and activities for each selection or group of selections. The teacher's guide provides additional detailed questions and activities.

- Selections for each book were made on the basis of their appeal, potential impact, and relevance for adult readers of both sexes. Every learner is sure to find a piece that connects with his or her life experience. The selections reflect the cultural and geographic diversity of adult readers. Many are written in the everyday language familiar to adult students. Sample themes for *Expressions* volumes 1 and 2 include: unrequited love; inability to communicate; growing into manhood; surviving divorce; becoming aware of the world outside one's community; maintaining one's integrity. Themes for *Viewpoints* volumes 1 and 2 include: achieving against the odds; realizing one's dreams; appreciating the lighter side of life; performing nontraditional jobs; adjusting to life in the United States; being a part of a family.

- Selections are *real* literature, not adaptations. All of the poems and stories in *Expressions* volumes 1 and 2 are complete and unabridged. While *Viewpoints* volumes 1 and 2 contain a few excerpts that can stand alone, most selections are complete articles, interviews, letters, or speeches. The material can be approached in a variety of ways, depending on the needs of the students. Pieces may be assigned individually based on interests or to an entire class for group discussion.

- The selections in each book provide identifiable contexts for learners. The thought-provoking nature of each selection is sure to stimulate interesting writing activities. The variety of readings on timely topics is certain to elicit the group sharing that builds self-esteem.

- Pre-reading questions that precede each selection in *Expressions* volumes 1 and 2 (or group of selections for *Viewpoints* volumes 1 and 2) effectively stimulate prior knowledge as a background for reading the pieces. The post-reading questions following each selection are effective springboards for writing activities and group discussion.

· ·

INSTRUCTIONAL DESIGN FOR CONTEMPORARY'S
WHOLE LANGUAGE SERIES TEACHER'S GUIDE

This teacher's guide was specifically developed for instructors with limited experience using literature-based reading material to teach reading. We have striven to create a "user-friendly" guide with clear-cut strategies. This book is set up so that the new teacher need only pick up the manual, open it to the appropriate page, take a few minutes to skim the plan, and begin. However, the lesson plan allows considerable flexibility for the teacher to deviate and improvise as class needs dictate. Features that make this guide easy to use include:

- lesson plans that guide the teacher/facilitator through each step of instruction, from giving the summary to discussing the piece after reading it to assigning writing activities

- a clear-cut division of the parts that correspond to the four individual student books: *Expressions, Volume 1* and *Viewpoints, Volume 1* lessons make up the first part of the guide; volume 2 of *Expressions* and *Viewpoints* is covered in the second half of this guide

- a two-page spread format for each story or poem (each theme for *Viewpoints* volumes 1 and 2) so the teacher can see the entire approach at a glance

- headings for each of the four components of the lesson boldfaced for easy identification: **Title** or **Theme**; **Summary**; **Step-by-Step Lesson Plan**; **Activities**

- post-reading comprehension questions that are identified in the guide by the following icons:

   L literal   **I** interpretive   **C** critical

- post-reading questions that are taken from the student books and are duplicated in the teacher's guide word-for-word; additional questions (not appearing in the student book) are in italics

- suggested answers given for each question to guide discussion

- writing activities that are identified for suitability to the experience level of the learner:

   B for beginning writers   **I** for intermediate writers

   E for more experienced writers

- suggestions for guest speakers, visual or auditory aids, videocassettes, etc., included as extension and enrichment activities

· ·

READABILITY LEVELS OF THE SELECTIONS

Finding high-interest material for adults written at levels lower than the eighth grade was a formidable task. With a few exceptions, the selections in the four anthologies range from the fourth through the seventh grade reading levels on the Fry readability scale. A couple of the selections fall below the fourth-grade level. Conversely, a few selections exceed the seventh-grade level. In these cases, we felt that the interest level of the readings, coupled with the adult learner's considerable background knowledge and experience, would help to compensate for the more challenging vocabulary and sentence structure. Obviously, in the final analysis, the teacher's judgment must be the determining factor in deciding the appropriateness of a selection. As an aid to the learner, we have glossed difficult or unfamiliar vocabulary at the bottom of the page on which it appears.

· ·

FIVE SELECTED WHOLE-LANGUAGE ACTIVITIES

Here are five activities that may be useful for implementing a whole-language approach with adult learners. Some of these activities use as stimuli selections taken directly from *Expressions* volumes 1 and 2 and *Viewpoints* volumes 1 and 2. For additional activities, you may consult the many books available for teaching reading strategies. At the end of this introduction is a selected bibliography of readings on the whole-language philosophy.

We hope that you experience the same excitement using Contemporary's *Whole Language Series* as we experienced conceiving and developing it.

SEMANTIC WEBBING, OR CLUSTERING

One technique to stimulate prior knowledge and establish a purpose for reading is webbing, or clustering: The teacher writes on the board an idea or concept related to the reading assignment and circles it. He or she then asks students for words or phrases that they associate with the circled word. Without censoring responses, the teacher records and circles each association and connects it to the central concept with a line. The graphic below is based on the Langston Hughes story "Early Autumn," included in the first volume of *Expressions*.

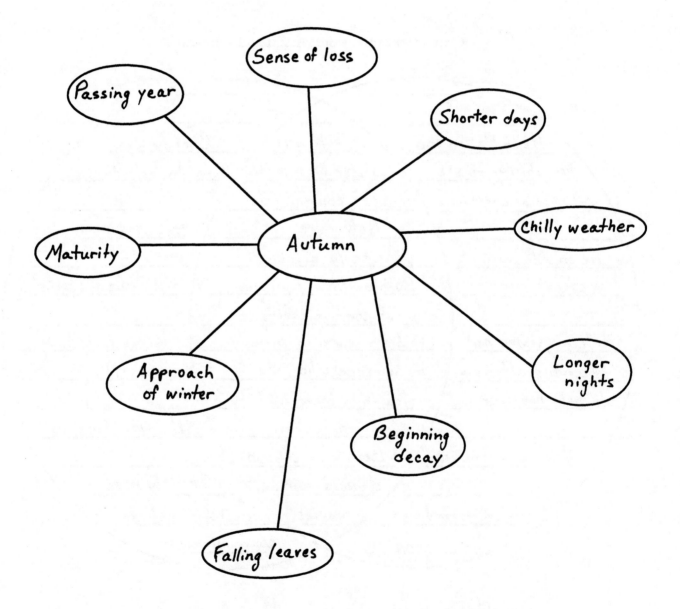

VENN DIAGRAM

A Venn diagram is a technique to graphically illustrate comparison and contrast. This visual technique consists of two overlapping circles: Similarities are listed in the small area in which the circles overlap; differences are listed in the larger areas on either side. These diagrams can be duplicated and passed out to the students to fill out or can be written on the board and used as a class activity. The Venn diagram shown below is based on two selections from "Great Moments," the first theme in the first volume of *Viewpoints*: Helen Keller and Christy Brown are compared and contrasted.

Characterization: Comparison and Contrast

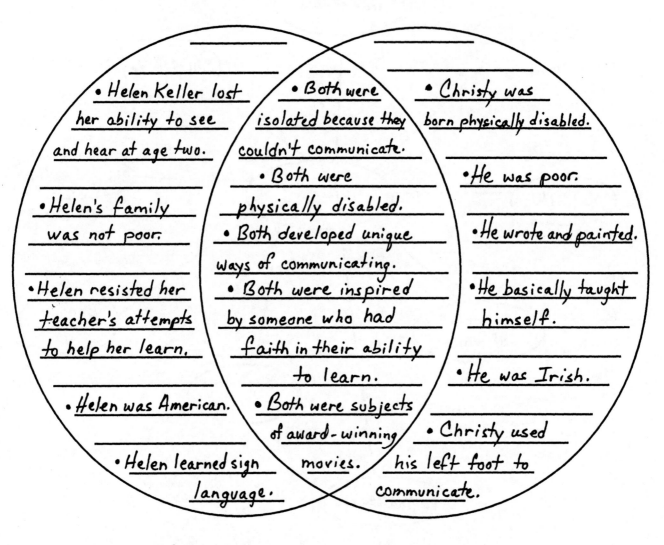

THE BARE-BONES STORY MAP

A chart showing four sections is drawn with each of the following four words as headings: SOMEBODY, WANTED, BUT, SO. As students read the story, they complete the chart, naming the main character, the character's goal, the conflict, and the solution. Here is the kind of information that each category might contain:

SOMEBODY	WANTED	BUT	SO
Character: (description of main character; relationships with other characters—friends, relatives; personality traits)	**Goal:** (when and/or where goal was established; why goal is important)	**Problem:** (how and/or why problem arose; ways problem could have been avoided)	**Solution:** (who provided solution; under what circumstances; other possible solutions)

BARE-BONES STORY MAP FOR "ONE THROW" (first volume of *Expressions*)

SOMEBODY	WANTED	BUT	SO
Pete Maneri, talented minor-league baseball player	a chance to play in the majors, with the New York Yankees	no one recognizes his ability	he is advised by a Yankees' scout to draw attention to himself by throwing a game but goes against the advice; when he does, he wins his big chance

STORY PYRAMID
Learners' comprehension and recall abilities are tested by having them list facts about character, setting, the problem, events, and solution from a story they read. Students build a word pyramid using story concepts.

STORY PYRAMID FOR "SEPARATING" (second volume of *Expressions*)

1. Michael

2. 13-year-old   boy

3. disrupted   small-town   household

4. unhappy   father   leaves   wife

5. father   dates   younger   woman   Darilyn

6. mother   begins   dating;   Darilyn   leaves   father

7. father   attempts   reconciliation   with   mother;   she   refuses

8. parents   and   son   must   adjust   to   family   breakup

---

1. Name of main character
2. Two words describing main character
3. Three words describing setting
4. Four words stating problem
5. Five words describing one event
6. Six words describing second event
7. Seven words describing third event
8. Eight words stating solution

STORY GRAM

Learners fill out a chart for a story they've read. The chart has six sections:
title and author, setting, characters, goal/problem, climax, and resolution.

(example from second volume of *Viewpoints*)

Title and Author	Setting	Characters
"The Parrot's Beak" Kartar Dhillon	mother's bedroom	mother and daughter
Goal/Problem	**Climax**	**Resolution**
Ill mother wants to reconcile with daughter.	Mother reveals she saved daughter from arranged marriage.	Daughter realizes mother loves her.

· ·

A SELECTED BIBLIOGRAPHY OF WHOLE-LANGUAGE MATERIALS

For your reference, the following books and articles about the whole-language philosophy are listed:

Goodman, K. *What's Whole About Whole Language?* Portsmouth, NH: Heinemann Educational Books, 1986 (79 pp.).

―――. "I Didn't Found Whole Language." *The Reading Teacher* (Nov. 1992): 12–15.

Kleslus, J. "What Is Whole Language?" *Florida Reading Quarterly* (Dec. 1988): 17–23.

Lim, H. L. and D. Watson. "Whole Language Content Classes for Second-Language Learners." *The Reading Teacher* (February 1993): 27–30.

Newman, J., ed. *Whole Language: Theory in Use.* Portsmouth, NH: Heinemann Educational Books, 1985 (224 pp.).

―――. "Myths of Whole Language." *The Reading Teacher* (Sept. 1990): 5–9.

Reutzel, D. and P. Hollingworth. "Whole Language and the Practitioner." *Academic Therapy* 23 (4): 405–16 (March 1988).

Soifer, R., M. Irwin, B. Crumrine, E. Honzaki, B. Simmons, D. Young, *The Complete Theory-to-Practice Handbook of Adult Literacy: Curriculum Design and Teaching Approaches.* New York: Teachers College Press, 1990 (212 pp.).

Yatvin, Joanne. *Developing a Whole Language Program for a Whole School.* Midlothian, VA: Virginia State Reading Association, 1991 (39 pp.).

Contemporary's Whole Language Series

EXPRESSIONS

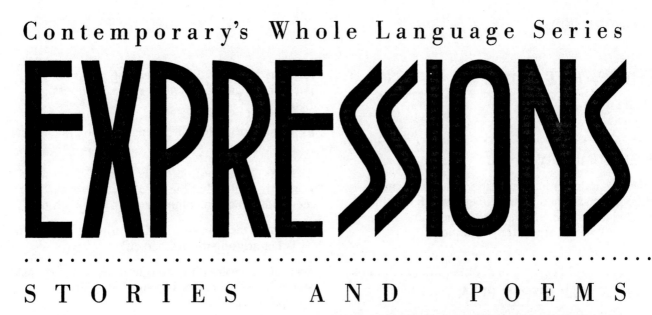

STORIES AND POEMS

THEY WENT HOME
(PAGES 1-3)

· ·

POEM SUMMARY

A woman talks about her relationships with men. Although many men admired her, none formed long-term relationships with her. After spending "one night, or two or three," they went home.

· ·

STEP-BY-STEP LESSON PLAN

1. Ask the pre-reading question:

   • How does it feel to love someone who doesn't feel the same way about you?

Start a discussion by describing a crush you had on someone when you were an adolescent. Ask students to describe how they felt in similar situations. On a chalkboard, list at least three feelings you and your students associate with unrequited love, such as sadness, anger, and loneliness.

2. Read the purpose statement aloud to help students set a goal for reading:

   • As you read, think about how the woman in the poem feels. Does she think, What's wrong with me? Has she given up?

3. Give students time to read the poem silently.

4. Ask the following literal **L**, interpretive **I**, and critical **C** reading questions. (Questions that appear in the student anthology are in regular typeface. Additional questions, which appear only in this teacher's guide, are in italics.)

L *Throughout the poem, the speaker talks about "they." Who are "they"?*

Answer: her former lovers

I *According to the speaker, men said "that never once in all their lives, / had they known a girl like [me]." Did the men intend the comment to be a compliment or an insult? How do you know?*

Answer: Given all the other favorable comments that the men made about the speaker, it is clear that the men intended the statement to be a compliment.

L *What did men say that they liked about the speaker?*

Answer: her careful housekeeping, pleasant personality, aura of mystery, smile, wittiness, and figure

I What is troubling the woman in the poem? How do you know?

Answer: The repetition of the phrase "They went home" indicates that the speaker is upset that the men didn't make a commitment to stay with her.

I What is the speaker's attitude toward men? What is her attitude toward herself?

Answer: Answers for both questions will vary. Ask students to give reasons to support their interpretations.

I Read the poem out loud, using your voice to show different feelings. The first time that you read the poem, make your voice sound sad; the second time, angry; the third time, sarcastic. Which of these emotions do you think the woman is feeling? How can you tell?

Answer: Students' answers will vary. Ask students to give reasons to support their choices.

C *Complete the last line of the poem. How do you know what the last line should be?*

Answer: The repetition of the phrase "They went home" in stanzas 1 and 2 establishes a pattern. Based on this pattern, the final words of stanza 3 would be "They went home."

5. End the lesson with activities that meet students' needs, interests, and learning goals.

· ·

ACTIVITIES

LITERATURE

Rhythm, Rhyme, and Repetition

1. To introduce students to rhythm in poetry, scan a stanza of "They Went Home." (See page 19 of this guide for a more detailed discussion of stanzas.) Write the first stanza on a chalkboard. Ask a student to underline the syllables that you *accent*, or stress, as you read the stanza aloud. Direct the rest of the class to listen to the rhythm, or "beat," of the poem:

They went <u>home</u> and <u>told</u> their <u>wives</u>,
that <u>never</u> <u>once</u> in <u>all</u> their <u>lives</u>,
had <u>they</u> <u>known</u> a <u>girl</u> like <u>me</u>,
But . . . <u>They</u> went <u>home</u>.

2. Ask students to snap their fingers or clap each time you read an accented syllable. Then read the poem aloud again. Students should see that the first stanza establishes the rhythmic pattern of the rest of the poem.

3. Ask students to list rhyming words in the poem. They are as follows:

   - stanza 1: wives / lives

   - stanza 2: clean / mean

   - stanza 3: lips / hips

Students should also note the rhyming third lines:

- me / mystery / three

4. Repetition also is important to the structure of the poem. Ask:

   - Which words and lines are repeated? How do rhyming words and repetition add to the music of the poem?

5. Follow up by asking students to select a rap song or other rhyming, highly rhythmic song. Write a verse of the song on the board. Then ask students to scan the verse, find the rhyming words, and note any examples of word or line repetition.

COMMUNICATION

Mixed Messages

1. Point out the mixed messages that men sent to the speaker of "They Went Home." Although their verbal messages to her were complimentary, they sent contradictory nonverbal messages by leaving her. Ask:

   - Which message do you believe, the verbal or the nonverbal?

Communication experts say that when verbal and nonverbal messages conflict, people are more likely to believe nonverbal messages.

2. Write the following messages on the board:

   - "It's great to see you and hear about what you've been doing."

   - "I'm not angry. I don't know why you think that I am, because I'm not."

Ask two students to role-play the messages. Out of hearing range of the rest of the class, tell the students that they should sound and look insincere as they deliver each message. After each message is delivered, ask the rest of the class:

- Did you believe what the speaker said? Why or why not?

End the activity by discussing ways to use body language to complement what is said.

WRITING

The following assignments may be done in or out of class. **B** designates an assignment suitable for beginning writers; **I**, intermediate writers; **E**, more experienced writers. (Assignments that appear in the student anthology are in regular typeface. Additional assignments, which appear only in this teacher's guide, are in italics.)

B The woman in the poem lists some of her good points—things that people like about her. Choose one of the following beginnings, and write about one of your own good points.

- My best quality is . . .

- People like me because . . .

- The quality other people most admire in me is . . .

I Imagine that you are the woman in the poem, and write a short "Dear Abby" letter telling about your problem. Then write a short letter back, telling the woman how to solve her problem. If you want, use the following beginnings to get started.

- Dear Abby,
  I have a problem
  with the men in
  my life . . .

- Dear Lonely,
  Here's what you
  should do to solve
  your problem . . .

E Should people get married, or should they stay single? Explain which you think is better, giving at least three reasons why.

E *What does the woman in the poem wish would happen? What does she want out of life? Explain.*

EARLY AUTUMN

(PAGES 5-9)

....

STORY SUMMARY

Former lovers Bill and Mary meet by chance on a cold fall afternoon in New York City. He is surprised to see how much she has aged; she longs to discuss their breakup but cannot find the words. After they part, Mary realizes that they forgot to exchange addresses and that she didn't tell Bill that she named her youngest son after him. (Note: "The Sunday News," pages 10–11, is about a similar situation—a person confronting feelings about a past love. It would make a good companion piece to this story.)

....

STEP-BY-STEP LESSON PLAN

1. Ask the pre-reading question:

   • What do you picture when you think about autumn? Falling leaves? Chilly weather? Shorter days and longer nights?

Start a discussion based on images that students associate with fall.

2. Read the purpose statement aloud to help students set a goal for reading:

   • As you read, think about the title of the story. Why does the story take place in the fall?

3. Give students time to read the story silently, or assign students to read the roles of Bill, Mary, and the narrator, and ask them to read the story aloud as if it were a play.

4. Ask the following literal **L**, interpretive **I**, and critical **C** reading questions. (Questions that appear in the student anthology are in regular typeface. Additional questions, which appear only in this teacher's guide, are in italics.)

L *List all the background information given about Bill and Mary in the first paragraph of the story.*

Answer: Bill and Mary had been in love when Bill was very young. They used to enjoy walking and talking together. After a spat, they broke up. Mary wed someone else, and Bill was deeply hurt.

L Why is it surprising that both Bill and Mary are living in New York City?

Answers: Both used to live in Ohio and, independent of each other, moved to New York City.

I Is Bill still in love with Mary? How do you know?

Answer: Several details indicate that Bill no longer loves Mary. He shakes her hand instead of kissing her, furrows his brow upon hearing that she lives in New York City, and thinks about how old she looks.

I The last sentence of the story says that Mary named her youngest son after Bill. What does this tell you about her feelings for Bill Walker? Is Mary still attracted to him? How can you tell?

Answer: Mary's naming her youngest son after Bill shows that she still loved Bill long after her marriage. Several details indicate that Mary is still attracted to Bill. For example, she lifts her face for a kiss, longs to talk about the past, and regrets forgetting to exchange addresses.

C The writer of "Early Autumn" could have had the story take place at any time of year and day in any kind of weather. But he chose to have Bill and Mary meet on a cold fall day as the sun is setting. Why?

Answer: Fall and chilly weather signal the end of summer, and the setting sun signals the end of day. The season, weather, and time of day support the situation depicted in the story—former lovers' realization that they cannot rekindle their relationship.

I Much of the story is dialogue—two people talking to each other. Try reading the story out loud, as if you were reading a play or a movie script. If you could make a movie of "Early Autumn," which actors would you choose to play Bill and Mary?

Answer: Students' answers will vary. Ask students to give reasons for their choices.

5. End the lesson with activities that meet students' needs, interests, and learning goals.

ACTIVITIES

LITERATURE

Setting

1. Point out that time is an especially important aspect of setting in "Early Autumn." Ask students to reread the story, looking for references to time of year, time of day, and time of life. They are as follows:

   - *time of year:* "It was . . . cold." "The leaves fell slowly from the trees in the Square." (page 6)

   - *time of day:* "It was late afternoon. Nearly sunset." "Autumn dusk." (page 6)

   - *time of life:* "When Bill was very young, they had been in love." "Yesterday, walking across Washington Square, she [Mary] saw him for the first time in years." "At first he did not recognize her, to him she seemed so old." (page 5)

2. Discuss how the time references support the situation depicted in the story.

COMMUNICATION

Withholding Feelings

1. Point out that lack of communication may have helped cause Bill and Mary's breakup. Instead of discussing their feelings, they stopped talking to each other.

2. Tell students to think of a time when they refused to discuss their feelings with a family member who upset them. Then ask:

   - Why did you refuse to discuss your feelings?

   - What were the advantages of withholding your feelings? The disadvantages?

   - If you had it to do over again, would you still withhold your feelings? Why or why not?

WRITING

The following assignments may be done in or out of class. **B** designates an assignment suitable for beginning writers; **I**, intermediate writers; **E**, more experienced writers. (Assignments that appear in the student anthology are in regular typeface. Additional assignments, which appear only in this teacher's guide, are in italics.)

B What do you think Mary would write in her diary after her surprise meeting with Bill? Imagine that you are Mary, and write a few sentences about what it was like to see Bill again. If you want, use the following beginning to start the diary entry.

October 1

Today I ran into Bill in Washington Square. It was quite a surprise to see him again after all these years. I felt so . . .

B *What do you think Bill would write in his diary after his surprise meeting with Mary? Imagine that you are Bill, and write a few sentences explaining what it was like to see Mary again.*

I It seems to bother Mary that Bill thinks she looks old. Write about a time when you changed the way you looked because of something someone said or did. What did you change? Your weight? Hairstyle? Style of clothes? Something else? Did you feel better after the change? Why or why not?

E Think of someone from your past that you would like to see again. What would he or she look like? What would the two of you do and say if you ran into each other? Write a short story about a surprise meeting between the two of you.

E Alfred, Lord Tennyson once wrote, "Tis better to have loved and lost / Than never to have loved at all." Do you agree with this statement? Even if a breakup is painful, is it better to have loved someone for a while than never to have loved the person? Explain what you think, giving examples to show what you mean.

THE SUNDAY NEWS

(PAGES 10-11)

. . . .

POEM SUMMARY

While skimming a Sunday newspaper, the speaker of the poem is shocked to read that a former girlfriend has gotten married. "Stung by jealousy," the speaker nevertheless clips and saves the wedding announcement. (Note: "Early Autumn," pages 5-9, is about a similar situation—people confronting their feelings about a past love. It would make a good companion piece to this poem.)

. . . .

STEP-BY-STEP LESSON PLAN

1. If your students are not used to reading Sunday newspapers, bring one to class. Demonstrate the combination of reading and skimming done by many newspaper readers, and explain that for many people, reading the Sunday newspaper is a leisurely, fun activity.

2. Ask the pre-reading question:

   • How would you feel if you ran across an ex-girlfriend's or ex-boyfriend's wedding announcement while thumbing through a newspaper?

Start a discussion by asking students to describe emotions they would feel and to explain why they would have these feelings.

3. Read the purpose statement aloud to help students set a goal for reading:

   • As you read, think about how the speaker—the person in the poem—feels.

4. Give students time to read the poem silently, or ask a student to read the poem aloud.

Ask the following literal **L**, interpretive **I**, and critical **C** reading questions. (Questions that appear in the student anthology are in regular typeface. Additional questions, which appear only in this teacher's guide, are in italics.)

L What first caught the speaker's eye while looking at the wedding announcements in the newspaper?

Answer: a former girlfriend's name

I *In the first stanza, the speaker says, "[I] missed the photograph." Who is the photograph of?*

Answer: an ex-girlfriend

I Was the speaker surprised to read that the ex-girlfriend had gotten married? How do you know?

Answer: The speaker was looking for something else in the Sunday newspaper and only "flipped by accident" to the wedding announcements. The speaker was therefore taken by surprise.

I Does the speaker still care about the ex-girlfriend? How do you know?

Answer: Several details indicate that the speaker still cares about her. For example, the speaker's stomach tightens while reading about the wedding, and the speaker wishes that the announcement had included more information about the ex-girlfriend.

C *Stanza 3 begins with three very short sentences. What is the speaker feeling at this point in the poem? How do the short sentences help convey this feeling?*

Answer: The speaker is surprised and angry. The short sentences help convey the tension that the speaker is feeling.

I *Why did the speaker become angry and throw down the newspaper?*

Answer: The speaker is "stung by jealousy . . . mind aflame" and hates the bridegroom, even though the man is a stranger. The speaker may also feel betrayed. (Other answers are possible.)

I Explain why the speaker decided to save the wedding announcement.

Answer: The speaker kept the announcement as a memento of the former girlfriend. Although the speaker won't read the announcement again (just as the speaker won't rekindle the relationship with the ex-girlfriend), the speaker cannot bear to throw the announcement away and sever all ties with her.

5. End the lesson with activities that meet students' needs, interests, and learning goals.

··

ACTIVITIES

LITERATURE

Stanzas and Rhyme

1. Explain that the poem is divided into five units, or stanzas. Ask students to summarize the main idea of each stanza so that they can see the logic underlying the stanza breaks.

2. Analyze the use of rhyme in the poem. Students should see that the second and fourth lines of each stanza rhyme. Ask:

   • How does rhyme add to the music of the poem?

Follow up by asking students to paraphrase a stanza and then compare it to the original. Ask:

• Which version sounds better? Why?

COMMUNICATION

Conveying Bad News

1. Point out that people are sometimes more emotional about bad news when it takes them by surprise. Ask:

   • Would it have been easier for the speaker of "The Sunday News" to accept the ex-girlfriend's marriage if the speaker hadn't been taken by surprise? If the speaker had learned about the wedding from a friend rather than from the newspaper?

2. Use students' answers as springboards for discussing effective ways to convey bad news. Tell students to imagine that they are about to be laid off from a job that they need and like. Ask:

   • Which would you prefer: to be told the news in a private, face-to-face meeting with your boss or to read the bad news on a bulletin-board announcement?

3. Follow up by listing three methods for conveying bad news: in person, in writing, and by telephone. Then ask students which of the three methods they would use to convey the following messages and to explain why they prefer one method over another in each situation.

   • informing a landlord about a leaky roof

   • ending a relationship with a spouse or friend

   • giving an employer two weeks' notice

WRITING

The following assignments may be done in or out of class. **B** designates an assignment suitable for beginning writers; **I**, intermediate writers; **E**, more experienced writers. (Assignments that appear in the student anthology are in regular typeface. Additional assignments, which appear only in this teacher's guide, are in italics.)

B What would happen if the speaker of "The Sunday News" called the ex-girlfriend? What do you think they would say to each other? Write a conversation for the two.

I Many people like to keep mementos of important events in their lives. For example, a business owner might frame the first dollar his or her company earns. Or parents might bronze their child's first pair of shoes. Describe a memento that you have kept for a long time, and tell why it is important to you.

E Why do people put announcements of their wedding in the newspaper? Explain why you would—or would not—choose to have your wedding reported in your local paper.

E *Read "Early Autumn," pages 5–9. Then compare and contrast the man in the story to the speaker of the poem. How are their reactions to their ex-girlfriends similar? How are they different?*

E *At the end of the poem, the speaker clips and saves the wedding announcement. What do you think the speaker does next? Write another stanza for the poem, and describe what the speaker does after putting the announcement away.*

ONE THROW

(PAGES 13-21)

· ·

STORY SUMMARY

Eddie Brown, a New York Yankees scout, tells about the time he went to watch young Pete Maneri play in the minor leagues. To test Maneri's character, Eddie posed as a hardware salesman and suggested that Pete "throw" a game. Pete couldn't bring himself to cheat. He thus won Eddie's respect and a big break into the majors.

· ·

STEP-BY-STEP LESSON PLAN

1. Ask the pre-reading question:

   • Have you ever wished for a lucky break that would change your life?

   Start a discussion by sharing a story about a lucky break you have had, or ask students to describe a lucky break that they would like to receive.

2. Read the purpose statement aloud to help students set a goal for reading:

   • As you read the story, think about the title. What is the "one throw" the title refers to?

3. Give students time to read the story silently, or assign students to read the roles of Eddie Brown, the hotel desk manager, and Pete Maneri as if the story were a play.

4. Ask the following literal **L**, interpretive **I**, and critical **C** reading questions. (Questions that appear in the student anthology are in regular typeface. Additional questions, which appear only in this teacher's guide, are in italics.)

L Pete seems eager to know if he received any mail. What letter is he hoping to receive?

Answer: a letter from the major leagues

L Who does Eddie Brown pretend to be?

Answer: Harry Franklin, a hardware salesman

I Why does Eddie pretend to be someone else?

Answer: Eddie does not want Pete to know that he is a scout. He wants to get to know Pete and test his integrity.

L *Who is Al Dall? What does Pete think of him?*

Answer: Dall is the manager of Pete's minor-league team. Pete is disappointed that Dall hasn't been a stronger advocate for him with the majors. He therefore has a low opinion of Dall.

I *Is Pete a good ballplayer? How do you know?*

Answer: Pete's statistics indicate that he is a good player. He is hitting .365 and leading the league in stolen bases. He also says, "nobody can field with me."

I Eddie tells Pete about a way to get management's attention. What does Eddie tell Pete to do?

Answer: Eddie tells Pete to throw a game or two so that Dall will ask upper management to get Pete off the team. In this way, Pete will come to management's attention.

I Eddie's advice to Pete can be seen as a kind of test. What is Eddie testing?

Answer: Eddie wants to see if Pete loves the game more than himself and is testing Pete's integrity.

I Does Pete pass Eddie's test? Why or why not?

Answer: Pete passes the test when he cannot bring himself to throw a game.

C Were you surprised by the ending of the story? Why or why not?

Answer: Some students may have been surprised. Others may have anticipated the ending by noting foreshadowing, or clues to the outcome of the story.

5. End the lesson with activities that meet students' needs, interests, and learning goals.

ACTIVITIES

LITERATURE

Foreshadowing

1. Ask students whether they guessed that "Harry Franklin" was really Eddie Brown. Point out that writers sometimes *foreshadow*, or hint at, the outcome of a story.

2. Ask students to reread the story, looking for clues to Harry's real identity. They are as follows:

   - Harry asks probing questions about Pete.

   - Harry says that he recognizes Pete from pictures that he's seen.

   - Harry says that he used to play baseball, and he seems to have firsthand knowledge about baseball management.

   - Harry has a few drinks with Pete and shows a special interest in him.

   - Pete mentions that he doesn't know what Eddie Brown looks like.

   - Harry quickly changes the subject when Pete asks him what he does for a living.

   - Just before revealing who he is, Harry says, "I never got more of a kick out of anything in my life."

COMMUNICATION

Decision Making

1. Explain that "One Throw" is about a young man who has a difficult choice to make. He can throw a game to draw attention to himself, or he can play to the best of his abilities but risk management's ignoring him.

2. Divide the class into three groups. Give each group one of the following situations to discuss:

   - You walk into your family's business and see your favorite uncle taking money from the cash register. What should you do?

   - While driving in a car with a friend, you see your son (or daughter) talking to someone who is rumored to be a drug dealer. What should you do?

   - You need to sell your car to get cash for a down payment on a new one. Your car runs fairly well, but it has 150,000 miles on it and is out of alignment because of a recent accident. A friend says you can get a better price for the car if you don't mention the accident and if you turn back the odometer to 75,000 miles. What should you do?

Groups should list options and reach agreement about what to do in each situation. Groups should also give reasons for their decision. If groups cannot reach agreement, ask dissenting group members to explain their points of view.

WRITING

The following assignments may be done in or out of class. **B** designates an assignment suitable for beginning writers; **I**, intermediate writers; **E**, more experienced writers. (Assignments that appear in the student anthology are in regular typeface. Additional assignments, which appear only in this teacher's guide, are in italics.)

B Pete Maneri is compared to the famous shortstop Phil Rizzuto. Who is a sports hero today? Write a short letter to your favorite sports star, explaining why you look up to him or her.

I Pete hopes to get a lucky break. What lucky break would you like to get? A million dollars? Your own business? Fame? Describe the lucky break you would like to get and how you would feel if you got it.

E To see what kind of a person Pete is, Eddie tries to get Pete to throw a game (lose a game on purpose). Is Eddie wrong to tempt Pete in this way? Or is it OK since, in the end, Eddie helps Pete? Explain why you think Eddie is right—or wrong.

E *Imagine you are Pete. Write a diary entry explaining why you didn't throw the game and how you felt when you learned who Harry really was.*

APO 96225
(PAGES 22-25)

. . . .

POEM SUMMARY

A young American soldier fighting in Vietnam writes letters home to his parents. He writes about what he sees, not about what he does. Finally, at his mother's insistence, he tells the truth about his war experiences. In response, his father asks him not to write letters that are so upsetting. (Note: "Letter from 1Lt. Sharon A. Lane," in *Viewpoints*, would make a good companion piece to this poem.)

. . . .

STEP-BY-STEP LESSON PLAN

1. Ask the pre-reading question:

   • Have you ever held back from telling somebody the truth to keep from upsetting the person?

To start a discussion, give examples from your own experiences.

2. Read the purpose statement aloud to help students set a goal for reading:

   • As you read this poem, think about the young soldier and his feelings toward his parents.

If your students are not familiar with the Vietnam War, show them Vietnam's location on a map of Southeast Asia, and briefly discuss major causes and effects of the war. Before students read, make sure that they know *APO* stands for Army Post Office.

3. Give students time to read the poem silently, or ask a student to read the poem aloud.

4. Ask students the following literal **L**, interpretive **I**, and critical **C** reading questions. (Questions that appear in the student anthology are in regular typeface. Additional questions, which appear only in this teacher's guide, are in italics.)

L What three facts about Vietnam does the soldier tell in his first letters home?

Answer: It is rainy and has monkeys and beautiful sunsets.

I Why does he hold back telling his parents about what is happening in the war?

Answer: He doesn't want to upset them.

I Why does the soldier's mother insist that the soldier write about the war?

Answer: She can tell that his comments are superficial and wants to give him the opportunity to confide in her and his father.

I Do his parents really want to know the truth about what is happening in the war? Why or why not?

Answer: Some students may argue that the parents want to hear about what is happening but are not prepared for the truth. Other students may argue that the father's response indicates that the parents do not want to know the truth about the fighting.

C We are given the soldier's address but not his name. Why might the poet have decided to leave the soldier and his family nameless?

Answer: The poem becomes more universal. Although it is about a soldier fighting in the Vietnam War, in a larger sense it is about the communication gap between soldiers and civilians in any war. (Other answers are possible.)

C *Why does the poem end with the line "Sure rains a lot here"?*

Answer: to show that the parents (and, by extension, the American people back home) would rather hear innocuous comments about the weather than the truth about the war

5. End the lesson with activities that meet students' needs, interests, and learning goals.

. . . .

ACTIVITIES

LITERATURE

Stanzas and Transitions

1. Ask students to explain the stanza breaks in the poem. Students should see that each stanza is about a different letter.

2. Ask students to underline the *transitions* at the beginning of stanzas (*but, and, to which, so*). Explain that these words connect ideas and show logical relationships.

3. Read the poem aloud twice. The first time, omit the transitions at the beginning of stanzas. The second time, include them. Then ask:

- What do the transitions add to the poem?

Students should understand that the transitions help unify the poem.

4. Point out that students can unify their own writing by using connecting words. Copy the following list on a chalkboard for students' reference:

- *additional idea:* and, also, in addition, moreover, furthermore

- *contrast:* but, yet, on the other hand, however, nevertheless

- *effect:* so, therefore, as a result, consequently

- *time order:* first, next, then, finally

COMMUNICATION

Silent Messages

1. Write the following saying on a chalkboard:

- You cannot *not* communicate.

Ask students to discuss what the adage means. Students should see that silence also communicates a message. Like the young soldier in the poem, people may communicate meaning by what they do *not* say.

2. List the following situations on a chalkboard:

- not writing back

- not returning phone calls

- not inviting someone to a party

- not complimenting someone on his or her new clothing or car

Then ask students to describe the silent message sent in each situation.

Empathy

Many communities have branches of veterans' organizations, such as VietNow. Build empathy for the young soldier in the poem by inviting a representative of a veterans' organization to speak to the class. To prepare for the visit, ask students to write a list of questions that they would like to ask. After the visit, ask students to present an oral or written summary of what they learned.

WRITING

The following assignments may be done in or out of class. **B** designates an assignment suitable for beginning writers; **I**, intermediate writers; **E**, more experienced writers. (Assignments that appear in the student anthology are in regular typeface. Additional assignments, which appear only in this teacher's guide, are in italics.)

B Soldiers enjoy getting letters. Explain why letters from home are so important to them.

I Write about a time when you held back from telling somebody the truth to keep from upsetting the person. Do you think you made the right decision? Why or why not?

I Like the soldier in the poem, do you sometimes hold back from telling family or friends the truth? Or are you a completely honest person in your relationships with family and friends? Explain which kind of person you are.

E The poem ends with the soldier writing a letter that says, "Sure rains a lot here . . ." What do you think the soldier's parents write in their letter back to him? Write a few more lines for the poem, telling what you think the parents say in answer to their son's letter.

E *How does the soldier feel about the war? Imagine you are he, and write a letter in which you reveal your true feelings to a close friend.*

TICKITS

(PAGES 27-31)

· ·

STORY SUMMARY

Toby Heckler, a disabled young man, lives by rigid rules and standards. When people violate his rules, he cites their offenses on handwritten "tickits." Although he gives tickets to strangers, he is unable to give tickets to the person he'd most like to change and control: his mother. The tickets that he writes to her remain undelivered.

· ·

STEP-BY-STEP LESSON PLAN

1. Ask the pre-reading question:

   • How do you cope when everything seems wrong?

To start the discussion, give examples of ways that you yourself cope.

2. Read the purpose statement aloud to help students set a goal for reading:

   • Toby Heckler has a very unusual way of dealing with his problems. As you read the story, you may feel as if you are breaking a code. You might have to read out loud to figure out what Toby is spelling. Once you know what words Toby writes, ask yourself, What makes Toby write tickets?

3. Give students time to read the story silently, or ask them to take turns reading the story aloud.

4. Ask the following literal **L**, interpretive **I**, and critical **C** reading questions. (Questions that appear in the student anthology are in regular typeface. Additional questions, which appear only in this teacher's guide, are in italics.)

L Toby writes and hands out several tickets. What does each ticket say?

Answer: parking mistake, too much in way, almost walked, tied wrong, Y broken, paper on grass, not listening, too much smoking, too much drinking, too much yelling, everything wrong

I Toby gives tickets to people when they make small mistakes. What are some other times in the story when Toby is picky about details?

Answer: ritualistic reordering of writing tools; meticulous printing; attention to cleanliness of shoes

I *Toby is mute, writes in "childish-looking" capital letters, and misspells common words. What do these details tell you about him?*

Answer: He is disabled.

L *Can Toby hear? How do you know?*

Answer: Yes. He seems to hear McVee, and he answers his mother's call, even though he is upstairs behind closed doors.

I Put yourself in Toby's place. What problems might you have if you could not speak? How might you feel about yourself? About other people?

Answer: Students will probably say that it would be difficult to communicate with other people and that they would feel frustrated with themselves and others. (Other answers are possible.)

L *Toby's last name is Heckler. What does* heckle *mean?*

Answer: to annoy with insults or criticism

I *Why does the name Heckler fit Toby?*

Answer: Heckler is a fitting name because Toby criticizes other people throughout the story.

C *Toby's only friend seems to be a police officer. Why is a police officer a fitting friend for Toby?*

Answer: Toby needs to feel in control. To fulfill this need, he follows rigid rules and standards and tries to make others do the same. It is therefore fitting that he be friends with an authority figure like a policeman. (Other answers are possible.)

I Toby writes tickets to his mother, but he does not give them to her. What does this tell you about their relationship?

Answer: It is strained. Toby does not feel free to tell his mother how he feels about her.

I Why does Toby write tickets?

Answer: Tickets are Toby's way of communicating with and exerting control over other people. (Other answers are possible.)

5. End the lesson with activities that meet students' needs, interests, and learning goals.

ACTIVITIES

LITERATURE

Characterization

1. Ask students to make a list of character traits that describe a family member or friend. Students should support each trait with "evidence"; e.g., "My friend Phoebe is loyal. I say this because she always stands by me no matter what."

2. Follow up by asking students to make a list of traits that describe Toby and to support each trait with evidence from the story.

Imagery

1. "Tickits" is filled with *imagery*—descriptive details that appeal to one or more of the five senses. Ask students to find and read aloud passages in which a color is mentioned. As students read examples, list them on a chalkboard. (For visual appeal, list examples in colored chalk.)

2. Follow up by discussing why the author includes so many visual details. Ask:

   - How do these details help readers see the world from Toby's point of view?

3. Have students think about meanings associated with colors used in the story (e.g., Toby's world view is simplistic. He judges actions as completely right or completely wrong. Toby's "black-and-white" world view is represented by Toby's white shoes and McVee's black shoes).

COMMUNICATION

Nonverbal Cues

1. Although Toby does not speak, he does communicate nonverbally, through facial expressions and gestures. Ask students to cite nonverbal cues described in the story and to explain what they think each one means.

2. Next, have students list nonverbal cues that convey the messages below. Students should think of facial expressions, eye contact, gestures, and body postures:

- "I'm interested in what you're saying."

- "I'm pretending to listen, but my thoughts are elsewhere."

- "I'm shy."

- "I'm confident."

3. Ask students to role-play the messages.

Perception

1. Educators have created empathy for the disabled by asking students to "walk a mile in their shoes." For example, students learning about the blind are blindfolded; students learning about the hearing impaired wear earplugs. Ask students to "be Toby" for an hour or two at home. During that time, they should not speak. Instead, they must communicate in writing.

2. During the next class, ask students to give an informal oral report about what it was like to be mute.

WRITING

The following assignments may be done in or out of class. **B** designates an assignment suitable for beginning writers; **I**, intermediate writers; **E**, more experienced writers. (Assignments that appear in the student anthology are in regular typeface. Additional assignments, which appear only in this teacher's guide, are in italics.)

B Who would you like to give a ticket to? Pick two people, and write a ticket to each person.

I Explain what you do to cope when everything seems to be going wrong.

I *Toby is meticulous about keeping his shoes clean and white. Write about something that you are meticulous about, such as some aspect of your appearance, work, or home.*

E Which are you: someone who likes to be in control or someone who likes others to do the controlling? Think of your relationships at home, work, or school. Then explain which type of person you are.

COLLECT CALLS

(PAGES 32–33)

. . . .

POEM SUMMARY

Three times, the speaker of the poem telephones his or her mother for help. Their lives and relationship deteriorate with each call. In response to the first two calls, the mother offers excuses for not helping. In response to the third call, the mother chastises the speaker, who is dying of a gunshot wound. (Note: Students might be interested to know that Diana Bickston wrote this poem in prison.)

. . . .

STEP-BY-STEP LESSON PLAN

1. Ask the pre-reading question:

   • Have you ever needed to phone someone for help in an emergency?

To start a discussion, describe times when you or a family member asked for help in an emergency. Focus on feelings that people have in times of need.

2. Read the purpose statement aloud to help students set a goal for reading:

   • As you read the poem, picture the two people talking on the phone. How do they feel about each other?

3. If your students are not familiar with collect telephone calls, review the procedure with them. Then give students time to read the poem silently, or assign students to read the roles of the speaker and the mother as if the poem were a play.

4. Ask the following literal **L**, interpretive **I**, and critical **C** reading questions. (Questions that appear in the student anthology are in regular typeface. Additional questions, which appear only in this teacher's guide, are in italics.)

L *Who is making collect calls?*

Answer: a daughter or son in trouble with the law

L What happened to the caller in 1979? 1980? 1981?

Answers: 1979—arrested and in jail; 1980—escaped from jail; 1981—shot and dying

L Why does the mother say not to call collect?

Answer: She has severe financial problems and does not have extra money to pay for phone calls. Also, she might not want to be put in the position of refusing a call from her child.

I *Does the relationship between the mother and speaker grow closer or more distant over the years? How can you tell?*

Answer: The mother and speaker grow more distant over the years. In 1979, the mother says she will write when she can, and she invites the speaker to call (but not collect). In 1981, the mother asks the dying speaker to repay a loan.

I *The call in 1981 is not a request for money. What is the purpose of the call?*

Answer: The speaker is calling to say good-bye.

I Do you think it would have made a difference in the caller's life if the mother had helped out? Why or why not?

Answer: Some students may argue that the speaker might have stayed out of trouble if the mother had been more supportive and helpful. Most probably will agree that a more supportive mother would have been a comfort to the speaker. (Other answers are possible.)

C *The poem is told from the speaker's point of view. How does this point of view affect how you feel about the speaker? About the mother?*

Answer: Students probably sympathize with the speaker rather than with the mother because the poem is told from the speaker's point of view. If the mother were the first-person speaker, students might sympathize with her.

5. End the lesson with activities that meet students' needs, interests, and learning goals.

ACTIVITIES

LITERATURE

Stanzas, Rhythm, and Rhyme

1. Have students compare the number of lines that the mother speaks in each stanza. Then ask:

   - Why do the mother's responses become briefer with each phone call? What does this tell you about her relationship with the speaker?

2. Have two students read the poem as dialogue between the caller and the mother. Direct the rest of the class to listen for rhythm and rhyme. Then ask:

   - Why do the mother's responses to the caller rhyme? Why do the mother's responses follow a more regular rhythmic pattern than the caller's? What do the rhyme and rhythm say about the mother's attitude toward the caller?

Students should see that the jingle-like rhyme and rhythm make the mother's responses sound insincere, as if she is reciting a list of excuses from memory.

COMMUNICATION

Roles People Play

1. Explain that a person may play many different roles in life. For example, an adult might play the roles of spouse, parent, employee, and friend. With each role come responsibilities. People expect a spouse, parent, employee, or friend to behave in certain ways. Ask:

   - What kinds of behavior do people expect from a good parent? Does the mother in the poem live up to these expectations?

2. Follow up by asking:

   - What happens when people do not follow the patterns of behavior associated with a role? For example, how do you feel about the mother in the poem?

3. End the activity by discussing role conflicts—problems that occur when the demands of one role clash with the demands of another. Ask students to describe conflicts that might arise in the following situations and ways that the conflicts might be resolved.

   - a person who is trying to be a good parent, employee, and student

   - a newcomer to the United States who wants to learn American ways yet preserve his or her cultural heritage

   - a new supervisor who must manage his or her former co-workers

WRITING

The following assignments may be done in or out of class. **B** designates an assignment suitable for beginning writers; **I**, intermediate writers; **E**, more experienced writers. (Assignments that appear in the student anthology are in regular typeface. Additional assignments, which appear only in this teacher's guide, are in italics.)

B Has there ever been a time when you really needed help, and it wasn't there? What did you do? Describe the problem and how you solved it.

I The mother gives several reasons that she cannot lend money to the caller. What would you say if your best friend asked you for rent money? Explain why you would say yes—or no.

E We are never told why the caller is in prison. Imagine what might have happened, and explain what the caller did to end up in jail.

E *We are never told why the mother is cold toward the speaker during their last phone call. Put yourself in the mother's place, and explain why you did not show more compassion toward the speaker.*

SPEED CLEEN
(PAGES 35-41)

· ·

STORY SUMMARY

Traveling home, Harry Joe Shreve leaves the turnpike to use a car wash in a town that he's never been in before. He watches his car go into the Speed Cleen Car Wash, but he doesn't see it come out. The surprise ending reveals that Harry's car was quickly disassembled for parts after entering the car wash. In an economically depressed area, the car-wash attendants are running a chop shop.

· ·

STEP-BY-STEP LESSON PLAN

1. Ask the pre-reading question:

   • Do you know people who cause problems for themselves because of the way they treat others? Maybe you've heard the saying, "That person's just asking for trouble."

Start a discussion by describing a troublemaker that you've known.

2. Read the purpose statement to help students set a goal for reading:

   • Something happens to Harry Joe Shreve's car at the Speed Cleen Car Wash. As you read, ask yourself why Shreve's car was "chosen."

3. Give students time to read the story silently, or ask them to take turns reading the story aloud. Help students visualize the setting as they read about it. On a chalkboard, draw a map that shows the proximity of the car wash, auto-parts store, and turnpike.

4. Ask the following literal **L**, interpretive **I**, and critical **C** reading questions. (Questions that appear in the student anthology are in regular typeface. Additional questions, which appear only in this teacher's guide, are in italics.)

I Imagine that you have been asked to help solve the "case of the missing car." Using clues from the story, explain what happened to Shreve's automobile.

Answer: At the beginning of the story, Shreve scolds one of the attendants for failing to remove a "V-shaped smear that looked like oil" from the left headlight of the Chrysler. After Shreve's car is missing, Shreve peers through the window of a nearby auto-parts store and sees a headlight "with a small, V-shaped black smear on the rim that looked like oil." Apparently, Shreve's car was disassembled inside the car wash, and the parts were moved to a nearby auto-parts store.

I *How does Shreve treat the first two attendants?*

Answer: Shreve is rude and arrogant toward the attendants. He calls one "boy," and he grabs the other to point out the oil spot on the headlight.

I Why didn't Shreve get a ticket? Who decided not to give him one?

Answer: The attendants decide not to give Shreve a ticket because of his rude behavior. (Other answers are possible.)

L *What state is Shreve from? How do you know?*

Answer: Shreve is from Alabama. The last thing he saw of his car was its Alabama license plate as it went into the clouds of steam.

I Why might the car-wash attendants prefer to steal the car of an out-of-towner?

Answer: It is easier to trick someone who is not familiar with the town and the car wash.

I Do you feel sorry for Shreve? Why or why not?

Answer: Some students may believe Shreve deserves the attendants' revenge because he behaved so arrogantly. Others may believe that Shreve is a hapless victim.

C *The name Shreve is a homonym for* shrieve, *which means "to atone for one's sins." Why does the name Shreve fit Harry Joe?*

Answer: Harry Joe pays for his arrogance toward the attendants with the loss of his car.

C Why is Speed Cleen a fitting name for the car wash?

Answer: The name has two meanings. It refers to how quickly cars are "stripped clean" as well as how quickly they are washed.

5. End the lesson with activities that meet students' needs, interests, and learning goals.

······························

ACTIVITIES

LITERATURE

Point of View

1. Explain that the story reveals the thoughts of only one character—Harry Joe Shreve. Ask:

   - How would the story change if the thoughts of the other characters were revealed?

Students should see that the surprise ending would be impossible if the reader could read the other characters' thoughts.

2. Follow up by asking students to describe what the story would be like if one of the car-wash attendants were the main character. Students might also enjoy rewriting the story from the point of view of one of the attendants. Ask them to write a short monologue revealing what the attendant is thinking during his first encounter with Shreve.

COMMUNICATION

Nonverbal Cues

1. Explain that people send messages about themselves through their style of dress, their possessions, and other nonverbal cues. The messages may be intentional or unintentional. Have students think about the nonverbal cues that show Shreve would be a good victim. Ask:

   - How do the attendants know that he has money?

   - How do they know that he is far from home?

   - How do they know that his car is in excellent condition and therefore good for parts?

2. Follow up by asking students to imagine that they are actors playing the role of Shreve. Have them describe the type of clothing they would wear and the gestures and facial expressions they would use to send the nonverbal message "I'm rich and arrogant."

WRITING

The following assignments may be done in or out of class. **B** designates an assignment suitable for beginning writers; **I**, intermediate writers; **E**, more experienced writers. (Assignments that appear in the student anthology are in regular typeface. Additional assignments, which appear only in this teacher's guide, are in italics.)

B Have you ever lost something valuable? Describe what you lost, and explain how you felt.

B *Many businesses have eye-catching names like* Speed Cleen. *If you owned a business, what would you call it? Name your imaginary business, and explain why you think the name is good.*

I Imagine that you are a new worker at the Speed Cleen Car Wash. What do you see happening to some people's cars? How? Why? Write a letter to a friend telling what really happens at work. If you want, use the following beginning to get started.

Dear Friend,
You wouldn't believe what's been going on at the car wash where I work. The boss makes money not only by running a car wash, but also by running a . . .

E Read a few police reports from a newspaper in your area. Then write a short police report about what happened at the Speed Cleen Car Wash.

MONTGOMERY

(PAGES 42-43)

. . . .

POEM SUMMARY

The poem explores the meaning of the Montgomery, Alabama, bus boycott, which was triggered by Rosa Parks's refusal to give up her seat to a white passenger. In a dramatic monologue, an African-American speaker explains to a white woman why blacks boycotted the bus lines. (Note: "I Have a Dream," in *Viewpoints*, would make a good companion piece to this poem.)

. . . .

STEP-BY-STEP LESSON PLAN

1. Ask the pre-reading question:

   • Can you really make a difference in the world?

Start a discussion by asking students to describe people who have changed the world for the better.

2. Read aloud the background information that accompanies the poem. You might also ask students to research the civil rights movement in a basic reference book, such as the *World Book Encyclopedia*. Students might give brief oral reports on the following topics:

   • civil rights
   • civil disobedience
   • Rosa Parks
   • Dr. Martin Luther King, Jr.
   • Mohandas Gandhi

3. Read the purpose statement aloud:

   • As you read, think about the people who took part in the boycott. For months, they walked rather than ride the buses. What made them do it?

4. Students may have difficulty reading the poem because of the line breaks. Read the poem aloud, emphasizing sentence breaks:

   • White woman, have you heard? She is too tired to sit in the back. Her feet two hundred years old. Move to the back or walk around to the side door. How long can a woman be a cow? Your feet will not move, and you never listen. But even if it rains, empty seats will ride through town. I walk for my children, my feet two hundred years old.

5. Ask the following literal **L**, interpretive **I**, and critical **C** reading questions. (Questions that appear in the student anthology are in regular typeface. Additional questions, which appear only in this teacher's guide, are in italics.)

I Is the speaker a black person or a white person? How do you know?

Answer: Several details in the poem indicate that the speaker is black. For example, the speaker addresses someone called "white woman," and the speaker says that he or she walks for "my children."

L *Who is the speaker talking to?*

Answer: a white woman

I The speaker says, "she is too tired to sit in the back / her feet two hundred years old." Who is the speaker talking about? Why does the speaker say the person's feet are two hundred years old?

Answer: The speaker is referring to Rosa Parks and—in a larger sense—all black women. The feet refer to two hundred years of oppression of African Americans in the United States.

L Why will "empty seats" ride through town?

Answer: Blacks taking part in the boycott will not be on the bus. Their seats will be empty.

I Why does the speaker say, "I walk for my children"?

Answer: The speaker hopes that the boycott will help end segregation so that his or her children grow up in a society free of racism.

C *Near the end of the poem, the speaker says, "but even if it rains empty / seats will ride through town." Why might the poet have chosen to end the line after the word "empty" rather than the word "seats"?*

Answer: The line break emphasizes the word "empty," underscoring the absence of blacks on the buses. (Other answers are possible.)

6. End the lesson with activities that meet students' needs, interests, and learning goals.

· ·

ACTIVITIES

LITERATURE

Stanzas, Rhythm, and Repetition

1. Although this free-verse poem is not based on traditional rhythm and rhyme patterns, it does have structure. Have students analyze the stanza breaks in the poem. Ask:

   • What is the main idea of each stanza?

Students should see that the poem is organized in logical units of meaning.

2. The language of the poem is simple yet powerful. Point out that the use of monosyllables slows the pace at which the poem is read, adding weight and power to the words. Ask students to underline all one-syllable words in the poem. Then ask a student to read the poem aloud, emphasizing the monosyllables.

3. The poem is unified by repetition. The last line of the first and last stanzas is almost the same. Ask:

   • What do the speaker and Rosa Parks have in common?

Students should see that the repetition of the phrase "feet two hundred years old" shows the common bond between the speaker and Rosa Parks. The speaker identifies with Ms. Parks.

COMMUNICATION

Perception and Listening

1. Ask students to imagine that they are African Americans participating in the Montgomery boycott. Students should describe, orally or on paper, why they participated and how they felt during the boycott.

2. Ask students to describe the boycott from Montgomery whites' point of view. Then ask:

   • What caused these two groups of people to perceive the same situation so differently?

3. Point out that the speaker in the poem says to the white woman, "you never listen." End the activity by asking:

   • How does perception affect people's ability to listen to each other? Is it easier to listen to someone you disagree with, or is it harder? Why?

WRITING

The following writing assignments may be done in or out of class. **B** designates an assignment suitable for beginning writers; **I**, intermediate writers; **E**, more experienced writers. (Assignments that appear in the student anthology are in regular typeface. Additional assignments, which appear only in this teacher's guide, are in italics.)

B Imagine that you are a reporter writing a story about Rosa Parks. Write a list of at least three questions that you would like to ask her in an interview.

I Rosa Parks helped change the world. If you could change the world, what would you change? Describe a problem you would like to see solved.

I *"Actions speak louder than words" is an old saying. Explain what the saying means, describing a few actions that have a greater effect than words.*

E "It is OK to break a law if the law is unfair." Do you agree or disagree with this statement? Explain what you think.

SHE SAID A BAD WORD

(PAGES 45-54)

· ·

STORY SUMMARY

Two women of very different backgrounds strike up a conversation on a Tampa, Florida, street. Lula, a young black prostitute, helps Mama, an elderly woman of Latin descent, carry home a torn bag of groceries. At first, the women make snap judgments about each other. But as they get to know one another, they change their attitudes. Lula needs a "mama," and Mama needs a daughter different from her own Vilma, who often passes judgment on her mother. By the end of the story, the two women reach a mutual understanding.

· ·

STEP-BY-STEP LESSON PLAN

1. Ask the pre-reading question:

   • Have you ever formed an opinion about somebody before you really knew the person?

Start a discussion by analyzing a common stereotype. For example, you might ask students to list characteristics young people often attribute to the elderly. Discuss how stereotyping affects people's perceptions of each other.

2. Read the purpose statement aloud to help students set a goal for reading:

   • In this story, two women with very different backgrounds make snap judgments about each other. How do their attitudes change as they get to know each other?

3. Students may have difficulty with the dialect used in the story. Read the story aloud so that students can hear the dialect, or ask them to underline unfamiliar dialect as they read silently. Then discuss the meanings of underlined dialect.

4. Ask the following literal **L**, interpretive **I**, and critical **C** reading questions. (Questions that appear in the student anthology are in regular typeface. Additional questions, which appear only in this teacher's guide, are in italics.)

L How do Mama and Lula meet?

Answer: Mama's grocery bag rips, and Lula helps her.

I *Which details first tell Mama that Lula is a prostitute?*

Answer: Mama has heard that prostitutes frequent the area. Lula's clothing, particularly her tight, leather miniskirt, makes Mama believe Lula is "one of them."

I *What bothers Mama about Lula's clothes?*

Answer: To Mama, Lula's clothes are immodest and impractical.

I *How does Mama react to being called Hispanic? Why does she react this way?*

Answer: Mama feels like objecting. She thinks of herself as a Latin and seems to dislike being categorized.

I Name times in the story when Lula is guilty of stereotyping—labeling people without knowing them as individuals. Does Mama stereotype people? Do Mama's neighbors? How can you tell?

Answer: Lula labels Mama as "one of these Puerto Ricans" and then as a Hispanic, calls white people "crackers," and assumes Mama leaves her purse unattended to test Lula's honesty. Mama stereotypes Lula when she thinks Lula's nose is "not what people expect," when she does not want to be seen walking home with Lula, and when she worries that Lula will steal money from her. Mama's neighbors are also guilty of stereotyping. For example, Alice implies that Lula is dangerous.

L *Mama wonders what her daughter would think of Lula. What details do we learn about Vilma through Mama's thoughts?*

Answer: Vilma is 50, single, "proper," and judgmental of Mama. Vilma is probably not easy to live with. Mama enjoys the freedom of being alone.

I *How is Lula different from Vilma?*

Answer: Lula is worldly and does not care what other people think of her.

I Mama's feelings about Lula change after the two women get to know each other. What does Mama think of Lula at the end of the story? What does Lula think of Mama?

Answer: Mama overcomes her prejudices and decides that Lula is "a good girl." Lula overcomes her prejudices and decides that Mama is a nice woman.

I *Why does Mama invite Lula to stay?*

Answer: Mama has begun to like Lula. Mama also feels sorry for her and wants to help her.

I Why does Lula turn down Mama's offer of money?

Answer: Lula may feel that Mama cannot afford to give her the money. In addition, Lula may wish to avoid being obliged to Mama. (Other answers are possible.)

C *The writer of the story had Lula speak in dialect rather than "standard" English. Why?*

Answer: The dialect helps characterize Lula and emphasizes the cultural gap between the two women.

5. End the lesson with activities that meet students' needs, interests, and learning goals.

· ·

ACTIVITIES

LITERATURE

Characterization

1. Although Mama and Lula come from different cultures, they have had similar experiences and are alike in some ways. Ask students to compare and contrast the two characters. Students should see that both tend to hold negative stereotypes about other cultural groups and both have been victims of prejudice.

2. Discuss how Mama and Lula build on shared experiences to overcome their differences.

COMMUNICATION

Communication Barriers

1. Point out that Mama and Lula have difficulty communicating with each other. Ask students to reread the story, looking for examples of miscommunication and barriers to communication. They are as follows:

   • To Mama, Lula is often "unintelligible" (page 46). Mama thinks that Lula doesn't speak clearly and dislikes Lula's use of "bad words." When Lula swears, Mama's "ears stopped functioning" (page 49).

   • Mama doesn't understand why Lula laughs when Mama asks, "Aren't you hot in that [sweater]?" (page 47).

   • Mama wants to turn down Lula's offer of help but is afraid to refuse "because the girl might misunderstand" (page 47).

   • Lula is sometimes put off by Mama's genteel manner of communicating. For example, Lula says, "And don't say my goodness . . . or I'll start in cussin'." (page 52).

2. Ask students to analyze causes of the above communication barriers. Students should see that the barriers arise from cultural differences.

3. If you have students who speak English as a second language, ask them to describe verbal and nonverbal communication barriers that they have experienced as newcomers to the United States. Then ask the class as a whole to discuss ways to overcome communication barriers.

WRITING

The following assignments may be done in or out of class. **B** designates an assignment suitable for beginning writers; **I**, intermediate writers; **E**, more experienced writers. (Assignments that appear in the student anthology are in regular typeface. Additional assignments, which appear only in this teacher's guide, are in italics.)

B Do people ever make snap judgments about you? Set the record straight by finishing these statements:

   • When people first meet me, they think I'm . . .
   • But once they know me better, they find out I'm . . .

B *Make a list of at least five slang expressions that are now in use. Then define each expression and use it in a sentence.*

I "You can't judge a book by looking at its cover." Would Mama agree with this old saying? Would Lula? Explain what you think Mama and Lula would say.

E What would Mama's daughter Vilma say if she knew that her mother had spent an afternoon with Lula? Write the conversation you think the mother and daughter would have as they argue about Lula.

NOTE TO THE PREVIOUS TENANTS
(PAGES 55-57)

· ·

POEM SUMMARY

The speaker, who has just moved into a house or an apartment, finds items left by the people who used to live there. Alone in unfamiliar surroundings, the speaker is grateful for the "continuity" that the items represent—the link between "the breaking of leases" and lives that have come and gone quickly, leaving little or no trace.

· ·

STEP-BY-STEP LESSON PLAN

1. Ask the pre-reading question:

   • Have you ever wondered about the people who lived in your home before you?

To start a discussion, describe items or other clues to the past that people have left behind in homes that you have lived in or offices and classrooms that you have used. For example, you might discuss a time when previous tenants' decorating taste was very different from yours. Have students describe similar experiences.

2. Read the purpose statement aloud to help students set a goal for reading:

   • The speaker of this poem moves into a home and finds items left behind by the people who used to live there. To the speaker, these items are clues to a mystery: what were the previous tenants like? As you read, ask yourself, What makes the speaker write them a note?

3. Give students time to read the poem silently, or ask a student to read the poem aloud.

4. Ask the following literal **L**, interpretive **I**, and critical **C** reading questions. (Questions that appear in the student anthology are in regular typeface. Additional questions, which appear only in this teacher's guide, are in italics.)

L Name the items that the previous tenants left behind.

Answer: cleaning supplies—soap, paper towels, mop, bucket

I What do these items tell you about the previous tenants?

Answer: The tenants had taken good care of the home. They may have passed on the cleaning supplies so that the new tenants could do the same.

I *Is the poem a thank-you note or a note of complaint?*

Answer: The poem is a thank-you note. The speaker says "thank you" twice and appreciates the care given to the home.

I *The speaker says that the previous tenants' lives were "a great wind that has swept by." In what sense were their lives like a sweeping wind?*

Answer: Like a sweeping wind, the previous tenants came and went quickly and left little behind them. The only evidence that they once lived there are the cleaning items, a hair in the sink, and dirt. The remnants that the tenants left behind lead the speaker to ponder the transient nature of life. (Other answers are possible.)

I The speaker thanks the previous tenants for "continuity." How does the soap create continuity between the speaker and the tenants?

Answer: The speaker bathes with a bar of soap used by the previous tenants. The strangers thus share a personal item and—in a figurative sense—touch one another.

C *The poet could have had the speaker be a homeowner who is writing a note to the previous owners. Instead, the poet chose to have the people in the poem be renters. Why is it important to the poem that the people be renters rather than owners?*

Answer: While ownership may continue indefinitely, tenancy is usually a temporary state. Since the poem is about the transient nature of life, it is fitting that the people be renters rather than owners.

5. End the lesson with activities that meet students' needs, interests, and learning goals.

ACTIVITIES

LITERATURE

Similes and Metaphors

The poet uses *similes* (direct comparisons signaled by the words *like*, *than*, and *as*) and *metaphors* (indirect or implied comparisons) to develop the poem. Ask students to find the comparisons used in the poem and to explain the meaning of each.

- "broom clean" (*metaphor*): The home is immaculate.

- "Your lives / were a great wind that has swept by" (*metaphor*): Life, like the wind, goes by quickly, leaving little evidence of its existence.

- "the dirt / seemed a gift, a continuity" (*metaphor*): The speaker is grateful for the remnants that the people left behind; they are a link between the past and the present.

- "soap, green in veins / like meltable marble" (*simile*): Although the soap looks as durable as marble, the soap—like life—will "melt."

- "soap . . . / curved / like a bit of an ideal woman" (*simile*): The speaker makes a personal item even more personal by comparing it to the shape of a woman's body.

- "I . . . / dried in the air like the floor" (*simile*): The image of the speaker drying in the air suggests vulnerability and, perhaps, the speaker's desire to feel the "wind that has swept by."

COMMUNICATION

Territorial Behavior

1. Point out that people tend to feel possessive about rooms and objects that they use often. Give the following examples:

- people who sit in the same seat every day on a bus or train

- students who sit in the same seat every class meeting

- workers who become upset if a co-worker uses their desk, chair, or office equipment

Ask students to give other examples of territorial behavior that they have observed.

2. Follow up by asking students to describe ways that people send the message "This space is mine." Here are some examples:

- posting "keep off the grass" signs

- surrounding property with hedges or fences

- filling an empty bus or train seat with packages so that no one can sit next to them

WRITING

The following assignments may be done in or out of class. **B** designates an assignment suitable for beginning writers; **I**, intermediate writers; **E**, more experienced writers. (Assignments that appear in the student anthology are in regular typeface. Additional assignments, which appear only in this teacher's guide, are in italics.)

B Imagine that you are packing a "box of memories"—items for your grandchildren to remember you by. Fifty years from today, they will open the box and see what kind of person you were. List five things that you would pack in the box, and write a sentence for each explaining why the item is important to you.

I Did people live in your home before you? What would you like to say to them? Write a short letter of thanks—or complaint—to your "previous tenants."

E Describe what it is like to walk through an empty new apartment or house for the first time. What do you think you might see as you walk through the place? What sounds might you hear? What odors might you smell?

E *Have you ever moved from one home to another? Explain step-by-step what people should do to make sure their move goes smoothly.*

THIEF

(PAGES 59-64)

. . . .

STORY SUMMARY

A man in an airport terminal is attracted to a black-haired young woman. After she jostles him in a crowd, he realizes she has stolen his wallet. When he finds her and asks for the wallet, she tricks him again. She gives him the wallet of her partner in crime, a blonde woman who runs up and accuses the man of being a thief. The man is arrested; the two women escape.

. . . .

STEP-BY-STEP LESSON PLAN

1. Ask the pre-reading question:

   • Have you ever been embarrassed by something that you said or did?

To start a discussion, describe a time when you were embarrassed, or ask students to describe their most embarrassing moment.

2. Read the purpose statement aloud to help students set a goal for reading:

   • The man in this story is made to look foolish by strangers. As you read, think about the title of the story. Who is the thief?

3. Give students time to read silently, or ask them to take turns reading the story aloud.

4. Ask the following literal **L**, interpretive **I**, and critical **C** reading questions. (Questions that appear in the student anthology are in regular typeface. Additional questions, which appear only in this teacher's guide, are in italics.)

L What makes the man first notice the black-haired woman in the airport terminal?

Answer: She has beautiful hair. He notices it before he sees her face.

L *When does the man realize that his wallet is gone?*

Answer: when he reaches for it to pay for a magazine

L The black-haired woman tricks the man twice. The first time is when she steals his wallet. What is the second time?

Answer: when she gives him the blonde's wallet

I What details tell you that the brunette and the blonde are working together?

Answer: Earlier, the man had seen the two women "deep in conversation." The women have planned a clever escape if one of their victims confronts them. The brunette pickpocket gives the victim the blonde's wallet. The blonde then accuses the victim of being a pickpocket and beckons a policeman. In the ensuing confusion, the brunette woman runs away.

I *The man could have told a police officer that the black-haired woman stole his wallet. Instead, he confronts the woman himself. Why didn't the man get help from the police?*

Answer: The man may have believed that he could resolve the problem himself. He does not seem to care whether the woman is arrested; he just wants his wallet back. The man may also have wanted to avoid the embarrassment of telling a police officer that he has been victimized. (Other answers are possible.)

I *What happens to the man after the blonde accuses him of stealing her wallet?*

Answer: The man is arrested and has to hire a lawyer to persuade the police of his innocence. His household is disrupted. The man feels embarrassed and angry. He thinks that for the rest of his life, he will "feel guilty around policemen, and ashamed in the presence of women."

I Why do the women return the man's wallet?

Answer: The women may feel guilty about stealing from the man and getting him in trouble with the police. On the other hand, the women may want to add to his humiliation. By returning his wallet with the contents intact, they are showing that they wanted only to embarrass and inconvenience him. Perhaps they want to punish him for eying attractive young women. (Other answers are possible.)

C *The writer of the story tells what the man is thinking. How would the story change if you knew what the women were thinking?*

Answer: If the reader knew the women's thoughts, the story would lack suspense. The reader would know that the women are pickpockets. (Other answers are possible.)

5. End the lesson with activities that meet students' needs, interests, and learning goals.

·····································

ACTIVITIES

LITERATURE

Character Motivation

1. Point out that it is important for readers to think about *character motivation*—the reasons that characters do what they do. Ask students to think of questions that they would like to ask the black-haired thief, the victim, and the police officer. Use the following questions as examples:

   • *black-haired thief:* What made you steal the man's wallet?

   • *victim:* Why didn't you get a policeman to help you confront the black-haired woman?

   • *police officer:* What made you believe the blonde's story?

List students' questions on a chalkboard.

2. Ask three students to play the roles of the above characters and a fourth student to play the role of an interviewer. The interviewer should ask the questions on the board; the other role-players should answer the questions in character.

COMMUNICATION

Perception

1. Point out that people may interpret the same situation very differently. For example, the man in the story believes that the black-haired woman "pretended to be attentive to him" and "blushed prettily" when he spoke in order to distract him. But there is very little evidence that the woman flirted with the man. The man's perceptions are colored by his attraction to her. Each person interprets events through the filter of his or her needs, desires, background, and experiences.

2. Ask students to analyze causes of differing perceptions in each of the following situations:

   • witnesses to a car accident giving different accounts of what happened

   • coaches of opposing teams arguing with a referee over a call

   • business owners complaining that employees are lazy and overpaid; employees complaining that they are overworked and underpaid

3. Follow up by asking students to describe times when they perceived a situation very differently from someone else. Have students analyze causes of the differing perceptions.

WRITING

The following assignments may be done in or out of class. **B** designates an assignment suitable for beginning writers; **I**, intermediate writers; **E**, more experienced writers. (Assignments that appear in the student anthology are in regular typeface. Additional assignments, which appear only in this teacher's guide, are in italics.)

B The man in the story is embarrassed by the theft. Describe your most embarrassing moment.

I Imagine that you are one of the women in the story. Write a letter to the man explaining why you returned his wallet and its contents intact.

E "Since the women returned everything they took, no harm was done." Do you agree or disagree with this statement? Explain what you think.

E *After being tricked by the two women, the man thinks that for the rest of his life he will feel embarrassed around women. Explain why the man thinks that he will feel ashamed.*

FIFTEEN

(PAGES 65-67)

. . . .

POEM SUMMARY

At the side of a road, the speaker finds a motorcycle lying on its side with its engine running. The motorcycle presents him with a dilemma. Should he give in to the impulse to drive away, or should he look for the owner? The poem captures the inner conflict of a fifteen-year-old torn between freedom and responsibility.

. . . .

STEP-BY-STEP LESSON PLAN

1. Ask the pre-reading question:

   • What comes to mind when you think about being fifteen years old?

Students may recall their teens as happy and carefree. If so, point out that for many, the teenage years are also a time of conflict. Start a discussion by describing a time during your teens when you felt torn between freedom and responsibility. For example, you might describe a time that you "cut" school or called in sick to work when you were actually well.

2. Read the purpose statement aloud to help students set a goal for reading:

   • As you read, ask yourself, In what ways is the speaker like a child? In what ways like an adult?

3. Give students time to read the poem silently, or ask a student to read the poem aloud.

4. Ask the following literal **L**, interpretive **I**, and critical **C** reading questions. (Questions that appear in the student anthology are in regular typeface. Additional questions, which appear only in this teacher's guide, are in italics.)

L The speaker finds a motorcycle lying on its side in the grass. How did it get there? What happened before the speaker came along?

Answer: The driver had an accident. He lost control of the vehicle, flipped over the guardrail, and was knocked unconscious.

L *In the second stanza, the speaker says that the headlights of the motorcycle are "fringed." What is fringing the headlights?*

Answer: the grass

I Does the speaker want to take the motorcycle? How can you tell?

Answer: The speaker wants to drive away on the motorcycle. He imagines what it would be like to "find the end of a road" or "meet / the sky on out Seventeenth."

I At what point does the speaker change his mind about taking the motorcycle? What do his actions tell you about him?

Answer: The speaker changes his mind after he imagines himself riding away on the motorcycle. At that point, he begins to think about the driver. The speaker's decision to look for the owner may be seen as a move toward adulthood. Instead of giving in to the impulse to drive away, the speaker acts responsibly.

I *The poem takes place near a bridge. What does the bridge represent?*

Answer: the teenage years, which bridge childhood and adulthood

I *The speaker does not cross the bridge. What would crossing the bridge have symbolized?*

Answer: If the bridge is seen as the teenage years, then crossing the bridge would have meant that the speaker had left childhood behind and "crossed over" into adulthood.

C The last line is separate from the rest of the poem. How does this affect the way that you read the line? How does it affect the meaning of the line?

Answer: The separation encourages the reader to pause before reading the last line. The pause, in turn, puts emphasis on the meaning of the line. By helping the driver, the speaker has shown maturity. Yet, in the end, the speaker is still too young to drive away and realize his fantasies.

5. End the lesson with activities that meet students' needs, interests, and learning goals.

·····························

ACTIVITIES

LITERATURE

Personification

1. Point out that the speaker *personifies* the motorcycle—describes and treats the motorcycle as if it were a human being. Ask students to find examples of personification in the poem. They are as follows:

   stanza 2

   • I admired all that <u>pulsing</u> gleam, the shiny <u>flanks</u>, the <u>demure</u> headlights fringed where it lay; <u>I led it gently</u> to the road and stood <u>with that companion</u>, ready and friendly. I was fifteen.

   stanza 3

   • We could find the end of a road, meet the sky on out Seventeenth. I thought about hills, and <u>patting the handle got back a confident opinion</u>. On the bridge <u>we indulged a forward feeling, a tremble</u>. I was fifteen.

2. Follow up by asking students to discuss how personification helps develop the theme of the poem. Students should see that the personification shows the dual nature of the speaker. While it is typical of children to personify inanimate objects, the sensuality of the speaker's descriptions is more typical of an adult.

COMMUNICATION

Denotation and Connotation

1. "Fifteen" is filled with language rich in connotative meaning. Point out that most words have both *denotations* (dictionary definitions) and *connotations* (ideas or emotions associated with denotations). To illustrate the difference between the two types of meaning, have students discuss the denotations and connotations of "cheap" and "inexpensive."

2. Ask students to discuss the denotations and connotations of the following descriptions from "Fifteen":

   • "pulsing gleam"

   • "shiny flanks"

   • "demure headlights"

3. Follow up by having students underline descriptive passages in brochures or ads for motorcycles and cars. Ask:

   • What message is the advertiser trying to communicate through word connotation?

WRITING

The following assignments may be done in or out of class. **B** designates an assignment suitable for beginning writers; **I**, intermediate writers; **E**, more experienced writers. (Assignments that appear in the student anthology are in regular typeface. Additional assignments, which appear only in this teacher's guide, are in italics.)

B What is it like being fifteen years old? Choose one of the following beginnings, and write about your teenage years.

   • I would like to be fifteen again, because . . .

   • I would not like to be fifteen again, because . . .

   • The worst thing about being fifteen was . . .

   • The best thing about being fifteen was . . .

I Like the speaker, most people feel torn between freedom and responsibility from time to time. Imagine that you have suddenly been freed of all responsibilities. Where would you go? What would you do?

I *When did you first realize that you had become an adult? Describe an incident or experience that made you realize you were no longer a child but an adult with responsibilities.*

E What does it mean to be mature? Write a definition for the word, and give two or three examples to explain your definition.

NORTH LIGHT

(PAGES 69-75)

· ·

STORY SUMMARY

A group of Israeli soldiers is awaiting a ground battle with Syrian soldiers. The soldiers were called up in the morning; as the story opens, it is afternoon. The speaker describes the soldiers' fears and frustrations as they wait to fight. (Note: "Letters and Verses About War," in *Viewpoints*, would make good companion pieces to this story.)

· ·

STEP-BY-STEP LESSON PLAN

1. Ask the pre-reading question:

   • How does it feel to face up to a fear and overcome it?

   Start a discussion by describing a fear that you once had. Ask students to describe the physical and mental effects of fear, such as sweaty palms, increased heartbeat, and sense of panic.

2. Read the purpose statement aloud to help students set a goal for reading:

   • As you read, put yourself in the soldiers' place. Picture what they see and feel as they wait to fight.

3. If your students are not familiar with the conflicts between Israel and surrounding Arab nations, provide background information for the story. Point out the locations of Israel and Syria on a map of the Middle East, and discuss major causes of the conflicts. Although the story probably takes place during the early 1970s, the situation depicted in the story may remind students of the 1991 Persian Gulf War.

4. Give students time to read silently, or ask students to take turns reading the story aloud.

5. Ask the following literal **L**, interpretive **I**, and critical **C** reading questions. (Questions that appear in the student anthology are in regular typeface. Additional questions, which appear only in this teacher's guide, are in italics.)

L When were the men "called up" to fight; i.e., brought to the battlefield?

Answer: on the morning of the day that the story takes place

L *What time of day is it as the story begins?*

Answer: afternoon

I Why are the soldiers being held back from battle? How do they feel about being held back? Why?

Answer: The soldiers are being held back until nightfall so that they can fight under the cover of darkness. They are outnumbered and have far fewer tanks than the enemy. The speaker says that the soldiers are angry about being held back because it is bad luck. Waiting causes anxiety; it gives the men time to worry.

I Though all the soldiers are frightened, the fears of the married soldiers are different from the fears of the unmarried soldiers. Why?

Answer: The married men are worried about their wives and children. The married soldiers are also older and more experienced. They have been in battles before and know what awaits them. The unmarried soldiers' fear is akin to that of "members of a sports team before an important match . . . for they are responsible only to themselves."

I *Does the speaker feel that it is necessary to be angry to go into battle? Why?*

Answer: The speaker says that the secret of being courageous in battle is to be angry. Anger gives the soldiers the energy and motivation to fight.

I When do the men finally go into battle? Why does the speaker say, "It is the right time; they've caught us at the right time."

Answer: The men begin to fight some time between two o'clock and three o'clock. The speaker feels that it is the right time to fight because the men are angry and ready. By five o'clock, they would be worn out by waiting.

I *What is the north light?*

Answer: The soldiers are on the southern ridge of a valley. The north light is the illumination from explosions occurring in the battle to the north of them. (Other answers are possible.)

C *The writer put the story in the present tense. What effect does this verb tense have on the story?*

Answer: The present tense gives the story immediacy. This verb tense encourages readers to identify with the soldiers and feel the same tension that they feel.

· ·

ACTIVITIES

LITERATURE

Conflict

1. Explain that there are two major kinds of conflict in literature—external and internal. *External conflicts* are physical or verbal struggles between two or more characters or a physical struggle between a character and a force of nature. *Internal conflicts* are psychological struggles. These inner struggles may involve the conscience or conflicting emotions. External conflicts often cause internal conflicts.

2. Ask students to describe the major external conflict in the story and the internal conflicts that it triggers. Follow up by having students explain how the internal conflicts are resolved.

COMMUNICATION

TV and Perceptions of War

1. Television brought the 1991 Persian Gulf War into America's living rooms. It is likely that your students watched some of the live broadcasts from the Middle East. Use students' recollections to discuss ways that TV helped to shape Americans' perceptions of the war. The following questions will help generate analysis and discussion:

- Some critics believe that TV news coverage made the war more acceptable to Americans by diverting them from the realities of war. These critics point to "packaging techniques" such as the use of dramatic theme music, eye-catching logos and graphics, and attractive young reporters. What do you think? Did TV news coverage bring the war closer to home, or did it distance Americans from the realities of war by making it seem like just another TV drama?

- Although some American news programs tried to give the Iraqi perspective of the war, most of our programs presented the point of view of America and its allies. Do you believe that more coverage should have been given to the Iraqis' point of view? Why or why not?

- TV made Americans familiar with nicknames for artillery, such as "Scud" for the Soviet SS-1 and "Scud Buster" for the American Patriot missile. Why do people give nicknames to war objects? How do nicknames help shape people's perceptions of war?

WRITING

The following assignments may be done in or out of class. **B** designates an assignment suitable for beginning writers; **I**, intermediate writers; **E**, more experienced writers. (Assignments that appear in the student anthology are in regular typeface. Additional assignments, which appear only in this teacher's guide, are in italics.)

B The story describes the effects of fear. Have you ever been really afraid? How did you react? Describe what you were afraid of and how you felt.

I Imagine that you are a married soldier waiting for battle. What would you like to say to your wife or husband? To your children? Write a short letter to them, explaining how you feel.

E The soldiers in the story are fighting to protect their homeland. What cause—if any—would you fight for? To protect your country? To protect your family? To protect your home or possessions? Explain.

E *Did you or any of your family members or friends serve in the military during Operation Desert Storm? Describe how you felt when you heard that war had broken out between America and Iraq.*

THE DREAM

(PAGES 76-77)

. . . .

POEM SUMMARY

A wife tells her husband that he "threshed and muttered" in his sleep. "What was it you were dreaming?" she asks. The speaker lies and says that he doesn't remember; then he asks, "What did I say?" She says that she "couldn't make out a word." But she, too, may be lying. Both are uneasy as he keeps his secret—to protect both himself and her.

. . . .

STEP-BY-STEP LESSON PLAN

1. Ask the pre-reading question:

   • Do you remember your dreams after you wake up?

Start a discussion by describing an unusual or frightening dream that you've had. Ask students to describe dreams that they've recently had. Point out that people sometimes dream about conflicts they are trying to resolve.

2. Read the purpose statement aloud to set a goal for reading:

   • As you read, ask yourself, What did the man dream about? Why won't he tell his wife?

3. Give students time to read the poem silently, or assign two students to read the poem aloud as if it were a play. Students may have difficulty differentiating between the dialogue and the interior monologue (unspoken thoughts). After students read the poem, ask them to identify which lines the husband says to the wife and which lines he thinks to himself.

4. Ask the following literal **L**, interpretive **I**, and critical **C** reading questions. (Questions that appear in the student anthology are in regular typeface. Additional questions, which appear only in this teacher's guide, are in italics.)

L How did the wife know her husband was dreaming?

Answer: He "threshed and muttered" in his sleep.

I Do you think the wife understood anything the husband said in his sleep? Why or why not?

Answer: Because the wife says "I couldn't make out a word," students are likely to believe that her husband's mutterings were unintelligible. You might wish to point out that the wife, like the husband, may be feigning ignorance.

L The husband says that he can't remember anything about his dream. Is he telling the truth?

Answer: The husband's interior monologue—inner expression of thought and feeling—reveals that he is lying.

I What do you think the husband was dreaming about?

Answer: Students may mention problems such as marital infidelity, serious illness, or loss of job. (Other answers are possible.) Encourage students to explain their answers.

I The poem ends with the line "And we smile uncertainly." Explain the feeling between the husband and wife.

Answer: Both are uneasy. He may feel guilty about keeping the truth from his wife. She may be worried because she doesn't know what is troubling him. (Other answers are possible.)

C *Why is it important to the poem that we know the husband's unspoken thoughts?*

Answer: If we did not know the husband's thoughts, we would not know that he lied to his wife and that he is genuinely troubled by the dream.

5. End the lesson with activities that meet students' needs, interests, and learning goals.

· ·

ACTIVITIES

LITERATURE

Rhyme and Alliteration

1. Point out that the language of the poem is carefully chosen; the poet cares about the sound of the words as well as their meaning. Have students underline rhyming words in the poem. Students should see that the second and fourth lines of each stanza rhyme.

2. The poet also makes use of *alliteration*—the repetition of initial consonant sounds in words in close proximity. Use stanza 1 to illustrate alliteration:

   • "What dreams you must have had last night,"
     My wife exclaims with a smile.
     "Really, you threshed and muttered
       So loudly, for such a while . . ."

Follow up by asking students to underline words that begin with the sounds of w, wh, and m. They are as follows:

• *stanza 2:* made, my, mind, wake, what, were

• *stanza 3:* what, why, word, whimpered, way, will, was

• *stanza 4:* why, was, what, was

• *stanza 5:* would, weep, what, would, we

COMMUNICATION

Lack of Communication

1. Point out that the couple in the poem use verbal and nonverbal communication to conceal their true thoughts and feelings. Ask:

   • What feeling does a smile usually represent? Do the smiles in the poem represent this feeling? Why or why not?

Students should see that the smiles in the poem mask anxiety rather than communicate happiness.

2. The husband says very little because he doesn't want to reveal his thoughts. Ask students to underline the sentences in which the husband speaks to the wife. Then ask:

   • Why does the husband say less than the wife?

Follow up by asking:

• Why does the husband ask, "What did I say?"

Students should see that the husband is worried he might have revealed the contents of his dream while talking in his sleep.

3. End the activity by having students imagine that they are marriage counselors advising the couple in the poem. Ask the following questions:

   • Do the husband and wife communicate well with each other?

   • What marital problems do you think the couple might have in the future?

   • What advice would you give the couple?

WRITING

The following assignments may be done in or out of class. **B** designates an assignment suitable for beginning writers; **I**, intermediate writers; **E**, more experienced writers. (Assignments that appear in the student anthology are in regular typeface. Additional assignments, which appear only in this teacher's guide, are in italics.)

B Use one of the following beginnings to write about a dream you have had:

• I recently dreamed that I . . .

• A dream I have often is . . .

• One dream that really upset me was about . . .

I The wife asks her husband, "What was it you were dreaming?" Imagine that you are the husband, and write about the dream you had.

E The husband in the poem wants to keep his dream private. Where do you go for privacy? Describe a place where you go when you need to be alone.

E *The husband is keeping a secret from his wife. Describe how you—or someone you know—felt while keeping a secret from a family member.*

ANDREW

(PAGES 79-87)

....

STORY SUMMARY

Roxie tells about the time she took Andrew, a newborn, from his young and incompetent parents, offering to take care of him until he was "good and strong." Roxie's hopes of raising the child as her own were dashed when the sheriff returned the infant to his family. In relating the incident, Roxie reveals much about her own life. She is single, childless, and has lived alone since her mother died. When her mother was ill, Roxie took care of her. Andrew was her way of filling the void left by her mother's death. (Note: "Mama's Legacy," in *Viewpoints*, would make a good companion piece to this story.)

....

STEP-BY-STEP LESSON PLAN

1. Ask the pre-reading question:

   • Have you ever had to make sacrifices for the people you love?

   To start a discussion, describe a sacrifice that you made for a family member or friend. Ask students to describe sacrifices they have made and to explain what motivated them to make the sacrifices.

2. Read the purpose statement aloud to help students set a goal for reading:

   • As you read, notice the details that tell you what her [Roxie's] life has been like. Why does Roxie want to help other people?

3. Students may not know the meanings of some of the rural southern expressions used in the story. Read the story aloud, explaining the expressions as you read, or ask students to underline unfamiliar expressions as they read silently. Then discuss the meanings of underlined words and phrases.

4. Ask the following literal **L**, interpretive **I**, and critical **C** reading questions. (Questions that appear in the student anthology are in regular typeface. Additional questions, which appear only in this teacher's guide, are in italics.)

L *Where was Roxie going when she first met Andrew and his parents? Why was she going there?*

Answer: Roxie was on her way to the home of a "white lady," who had hired Roxie to help set ducks.

L Who are Andrew's parents?

Answer: Andrew's mother is the granddaughter of Mrs. Littell, a woman who lives in the community. His father is a soldier who, in Roxie's opinion, is "apt to drift on."

I What made Roxie think that Andrew's mother couldn't take care of him?

Answer: She created a hazard when she built a fire in the middle of the floor on a piece of tin, and she did not have water or milk for Andrew.

I Roxie took care of her sick mother. What does this tell you about Roxie?

Answer: Roxie is a caring person.

I Mrs. Littell, Andrew's great-grandmother, says that Roxie is "backward." Mrs. Littell also seems to think that Roxie might have hurt the baby. What do you think? Would Roxie make a good mother? Why or why not?

Answer: Students will probably agree that Roxie would make a good mother. Several details indicate that she knows how to take care of an infant. She sterilizes the water used to dilute the condensed milk, feeds the baby with an eyedropper, wraps his abdomen in a warm sheet to aid his digestion, and makes sure that he can't roll off the bed. Equally important, Roxie genuinely cared—and continues to care—about Andrew.

I Roxie says she took Andrew to give him food and a warm place to live. But she also seems to have other reasons for wanting Andrew to live with her. What are they?

Answer: Roxie loves children. She would have liked to spend more time with her brother's children but couldn't because "Mama couldn't stand too much of their commotion." Roxie also misses taking care of someone. She says that Andrew was sent by God to take the place of her mother.

C *The story could have begun with Roxie's finding Andrew and his parents in the woods. Why might the writer have chosen to begin with Roxie going to set ducks?*

Answer: The incident establishes Roxie's character and foreshadows Roxie's taking care of the baby.

5. End the lesson with activities that meet students' needs, interests, and learning goals.

· ·

ACTIVITIES

LITERATURE

Characterization

1. To help students analyze the character of Roxie Stoner, stage a mock trial in class. Tell students that Roxie is on trial for kidnapping Andrew. Then assign students to play the roles of defense attorneys, prosecuting attorneys, and the jury.

2. Tell the prosecuting attorneys to make a list of reasons that Roxie should be punished for kidnapping Andrew. Tell the defense attorneys to make a list of reasons that Roxie should not be punished. Direct both groups to base their lists on evidence from the story.

3. Have the prosecuting and defense attorneys argue their cases before the jury. Then ask jury members to deliberate and defend their verdict.

COMMUNICATION

Stereotyping

1. As students read the story, it is likely that they did not perceive Roxie as "backward," even though there is evidence that Roxie is developmentally delayed. Because the story is told from Roxie's point of view, readers see events as Roxie sees them and feel empathy for her.

2. Ask students to name characteristics that they associate with someone who is developmentally delayed. Then ask students if the characteristics that they named apply to Roxie. Students will probably agree that the characteristics do not apply. Have students turn to page 86 of the story. Read aloud the passage in which Mrs. Littell reveals that Roxie is "backward." Then ask the following questions:

   • While you were reading the story, did you think that Roxie was developmentally delayed? Why or why not?

   • Would your perceptions of Roxie have been different if you'd read on the first page of the story that Roxie was "backward"?

   • How does labeling other people affect our perceptions of them?

   • How does seeing events from another person's viewpoint help develop empathy for the person?

WRITING

The following assignments may be done in or out of class. **B** designates an assignment suitable for beginning writers; **I**, intermediate writers; **E**, more experienced writers. (Assignments that appear in the student anthology are in regular typeface. Additional assignments, which appear only in this teacher's guide, are in italics.)

B Roxie is willing to make sacrifices for the people she loves. Write about a time when you made a sacrifice for someone you love. What did you sacrifice? Why?

B *Roxie would have liked to give Andrew a different name. Imagine that you have just been presented with twins—a boy and a girl. What would you name the children? Why?*

I What does it take to be a good parent? List and explain the qualities that you believe a person needs to be a good mother or father.

E Imagine that Roxie were arrested for kidnapping Andrew. If you were the judge in the case, would you punish Roxie? Describe why you would—or would not—punish her.

THE TELEPHONE

(PAGES 88-89)

· ·

POEM SUMMARY

The speaker of the poem says that his happiness is dependent upon an "electric appliance"—the telephone. In an impersonal world in which people are "separated from friends / By a tangle of subways and buses," the telephone brings "the human voice and the good news of friends."

· ·

STEP-BY-STEP LESSON PLAN

1. Ask the pre-reading questions:

   • When your telephone rings, how do you react? Do you get annoyed, or do you welcome the calls?

To start a discussion, describe your own attitude toward telephone calls. Explain how you react when the telephone rings while you are busy. Have students describe how they feel when telephone calls interrupt their work.

2. Read the purpose statement aloud to help students set a goal for reading:

   • As you read, ask yourself, Why is the speaker so happy to get phone calls?

3. Give students time to read the poem silently, or ask a student to read the poem aloud.

4. Ask the following literal **L**, interpretive **I**, and critical **C** reading questions. (Questions that appear in the student anthology are in regular typeface. Additional questions, which appear only in this teacher's guide, are in italics.)

L *What does the speaker's happiness depend on?*

Answer: an electric appliance—the telephone

I Where does the speaker live? Why has this location made the speaker dependent on the telephone?

Answer: The speaker lives in a city. As an urbanite, the speaker is "separated from friends / By a tangle of subways and buses."

I *How does the speaker feel about receiving telephone calls?*

Answer: The speaker feels joyous at the thought that he or she is "in the world and wanted."

I What "news" does the speaker get from the telephone calls he receives?

Answer: "good news of friends"—"love or gossip"

I The speaker says that without a telephone, "I was like a bear in a cave / Drowsing through a shadowy winter." Explain the comparison. In what way was the speaker like a bear in the winter?

Answer: Like a bear in winter, the speaker was "hibernating"—isolated and out of touch with the world.

I Do you think the speaker is often lonely? Why or why not?

Answer: Some students may believe that the speaker's dependence on the telephone is a sign of loneliness. Others may argue that the speaker isn't lonely because the telephone keeps him or her in touch with friends.

C *What is the tone, or mood, of the poem? How does the first line of the poem set this tone?*

Answer: The poet sets a light tone by juxtaposing an abstract, spiritual quality—happiness—with a mundane electric appliance—the telephone.

I *What do you think the speaker looks like? If you could choose an actor to play the role of the speaker, who would you choose? Why?*

Answer: Students' answers will vary. Encourage students to give reasons for their choice.

I *What do you think the speaker's home looks like? Is it a house or an apartment? What does it look like inside?*

Answer: Students' answers will vary. Encourage students to give reasons for their answers.

5. End the lesson with activities that meet students' needs, interests, and learning goals.

····························

ACTIVITIES

LITERATURE

Imagery

1. The poem is structured on contrasting images—spiritual or physical coldness and spiritual or physical warmth. (For a more detailed description of imagery, see page 25 of this guide.) Ask students to find images that fit each category. They are as follows:

- *coldness*

   "*separated from friends* / By a *tangle of subways*"
   "I was . . . *a bear in a cave* / *Drowsing through a shadowy winter*"

- *warmth*

   "My *happiness* depends"
   "Yes my telephone is my *joy*"
   "It tells me that *I am . . . wanted*"
   "It rings and I am alerted to *love*"
   "my hair . . . begins to *sparkle*"
   "It rings and *spring has come*"
   "I . . . amble out into the *sunshine*"

2. Ask students to explain the message communicated by the contrasting images. Students should see that they express the speaker's mood before and after receiving telephone calls.

COMMUNICATION

Silent Messages

1. Ask students to describe the nonverbal message sent in each of the following situations:

- being put on hold when you call

- being told that someone's phone number is unlisted

- calling a friend for help and receiving a taped message

- calling a business for information and receiving a taped message

2. Ask students to list ways that they can send positive nonverbal messages when they speak on the phone. Use the following list to generate ideas:

- Give the caller your complete attention.

- Smile as you speak; the caller won't see your smile, but your voice will convey a positive attitude.

- Do not eat, drink, or chew gum while talking on the phone.

WRITING

The following assignments may be done in or out of class. **B** designates an assignment suitable for beginning writers; **I**, intermediate writers; **E**, more experienced writers. (Assignments that appear in the student anthology are in regular typeface. Additional assignments, which appear only in this teacher's guide, are in italics.)

B When the electric power goes off, which appliance do you miss the most? Radio? TV? CD player? Other? Explain which you miss—and why.

B *Describe your attitude toward the telephone by completing one of the following statements:*

- *I like the telephone because . . .*

- *I dislike the telephone because . . .*

I Are you like the speaker, who waits for other people to call? Or are you the one who makes the telephone calls? Explain which kind of person you are.

E The speaker of the poem relies on the telephone to communicate with the outside world. Which of the following methods is your favorite way of communicating with friends? Explain why.

- telephone

- letter

- face-to-face conversation

BICYCLES, MUSCLES, CIGARETTES
(PAGES 91-104)

· ·

STORY SUMMARY

Two days after Evan Hamilton stops smoking, he must react as a rational, responsible parent. His nine-year-old son, Roger, along with two other boys, has been accused of destroying another boy's bicycle. When the father of one of the boys gets "out of line," Mr. Hamilton wrestles him to the ground. Mr. Hamilton is ashamed that he lost control of himself; Roger is frightened by the violence but admires his father's physical strength. Both father and son ponder what it means to be a man.

· ·

STEP-BY-STEP LESSON PLAN

1. Ask the pre-reading question:

   - How do you define *manhood*? Strength? Maturity? A sense of responsibility toward other people?

   To start a discussion, define *manhood*. Then ask students to list characteristics that they associate with the word.

2. Read the purpose statement aloud to help students set a goal for reading:

   - As you read, think about the men and boys in the story. How do the males show they are "men"?

3. Give students time to read the story silently, or ask them to take turns reading the story aloud.

4. Students may have difficulty identifying and remembering the characters in the story. Write the following chart on a chalkboard for reference:

   - *Evan and Ann Hamilton:* parents of Roger

   - *Unnamed boy who summons Mr. Hamilton:* brother of Gilbert Miller, whose bike is missing

   - *Kip Hollister:* boy who has a paper route; friend of Roger

   - *Mrs. Miller:* mother of Gilbert

   - *Gary Berman:* boy sitting on the drainboard in the Miller kitchen; participated in bike rolling

   - *Mr. Berman:* father of Gary

5. Ask the following literal **L**, interpretive **I**, and critical **C** reading questions. (Questions that appear in the student anthology are in regular typeface. Additional questions, which appear only in this teacher's guide, are in italics.)

L *What habit is Mr. Hamilton trying to break?*

Answer: cigarette smoking

I *How might Mr. Hamilton's struggle to break the habit affect his behavior?*

Answer: It might make him feel irritable.

I *What questions does Mr. Hamilton ask when the Miller boy summons him? What do these questions tell you about Mr. Hamilton?*

Answer: "What is it? Is it Roger? . . . he's all right?" Mr. Hamilton cares about his son.

L *Why has the Miller boy summoned Mr. Hamilton?*

Answer: Gilbert, the boy's brother, has accused Roger and two other boys of destroying his bike.

I *How does Mrs. Miller treat Gilbert during the discussion in the kitchen? Why?*

Answer: She treats him brusquely; she does not listen to him and warns him to be quiet when he suggests a solution. She feels that he is a child intruding in an adult conversation.

L Why did Roger and Kip borrow Gilbert's bicycle?

Answer: They borrowed the bike so that they could deliver newspapers together on Kip's paper route.

L How did Roger, Kip, and Gary hurt the bicycle?

Answer: They rolled it and threw it against a goalpost.

I *Does Mr. Hamilton want a cigarette during the discussion in the kitchen? How do you know?*

Answer: Several details indicate that he would like to smoke a cigarette. His palms sweat, he reaches into his shirt for a cigarette, and he notices the hissing sound of a cigarette being extinguished in water.

I In your opinion, which boy or boys are telling the truth about what happened to the bicycle? Which boy or boys are lying? How can you tell?

Answer: Students are likely to believe Roger's version of events because the story is told from Mr. Hamilton's perspective. However, there is little evidence to support any of the boys' versions of what happened. Roger is, perhaps, the most believable, but his defensive behavior may make him suspect in some students' eyes. Students may also feel that Kip loses some credibility when he changes his story. And students may feel suspicious of Gary because of his secret meeting with his father.

▐ Why does Mr. Hamilton attack Mr. Berman?

Answer: Several incidents lead up to the attack. When Mr. Berman leaves the kitchen to hold a private meeting with Gary, Mr. Hamilton has "the feeling he should stop them." Mr. Hamilton is further annoyed when Mr. Berman returns and takes charge of the discussion. The final straw is Mr. Berman's verbal attacks on Roger. Mr. Hamilton feels that he must defend his son. He may also feel that his masculine authority has been called into question. And, because he is trying to quit smoking, he may be on edge and less able to cope with stressful situations. (Other answers are possible.)

▐ How does Mr. Hamilton feel about the fight he has with Mr. Berman?

Answer: Several details indicate that Mr. Hamilton feels ashamed. He apologizes to Roger, refuses to let Roger feel his biceps, and sits alone on the front porch before telling his wife what happened. In addition, Mr. Hamilton's decision to quit smoking shows that he wants to gain more control over his behavior. The fight shows a lack of control that may be upsetting to him. (Other answers are possible.)

▐ How does Roger feel about his father after the fight?

Answer: Roger has mixed feelings. He is frightened by the violence, but he also is proud of his father's strength and assertiveness. (Other answers are possible.)

▐ Why does Roger think about his grandfather?

Answer: After the fight, the boy feels a strong bond with his father, his masculine role model, and wants to know if his father felt the same way about his own father. (Other answers are possible.)

◪ *Why is "Bicycles, Muscles, Cigarettes" an appropriate title for the story?*

Answer: The title foreshadows and supports the theme—boys trying to act like men and men acting like boys. (Other answers are possible.)

6. End the lesson with activities that meet students' needs, interests, and learning goals.

· ·

ACTIVITIES

LITERATURE

Conflict

1. Review with students the meaning of internal and external conflict. (See page 41 of this *Teacher's Guide.*)

2. Ask students to list and describe the internal conflicts that led up to the major external conflict in the story—the fight between Mr. Hamilton and Mr. Berman—and the internal conflicts triggered by the fight.

COMMUNICATION

Roles People Play

1. Mr. Hamilton struggles to fulfill two conflicting male roles—the strong authority figure and the sensitive, loving father. Ask students to look for examples of each type of behavior.

2. The boys in the story also struggle to fill male roles. Ask students to give examples from the story of boys trying to look or act like men.

WRITING

The following assignments may be done in or out of class. **◪** designates an assignment suitable for beginning writers; **▐**, intermediate writers; **◨**, more experienced writers. (Assignments that appear in the student anthology are in regular typeface. Additional assignments, which appear only in this teacher's guide, are in italics.)

◪ Have you ever been upset by someone's violence? Describe a time when you or someone you know settled an argument with fists instead of reason.

▐ Roger seems both impressed and frightened by his father's behavior. Imagine that you are Roger, and describe how you feel about your father and his fight with Mr. Berman.

▐ *Recall a time that a parent or family member behaved in an uncharacteristic way. Were you surprised? Frightened? Explain what happened and how you felt.*

◨ After the fight, Mr. Hamilton thinks about his own father and how much they are alike. Which of your parents are you like? Write about the ways in which you are like one of your parents.

FILLING STATION

(PAGES 105-107)

· ·

POEM SUMMARY

A speaker is appalled and amused by the filth that permeates a small gas station. But then the speaker notices that someone has tried to instill a sense of beauty and order in the station. Marveling at the hand-embroidered doily, the wicker table, and the carefully arranged cans of oil, the speaker concludes, "Somebody loves us all."

· ·

STEP-BY-STEP LESSON PLAN

1. Ask the pre-reading question:

   • Is there a family-owned store in your neighborhood? In a world of chain stores, it can be nice to find a small business run by people in the neighborhood.

Start a discussion by describing a neigborhood place that you consider special. Ask students to describe neighborhood places that are special to them.

2. Read the purpose statement aloud to help students set a goal for reading:

   • This poem is about a gas station that definitely is not part of a chain. Picture what it looks like as you read.

3. Give students time to read the poem silently, or ask them to take turns reading the poem aloud.

4. Ask the following literal **L**, interpretive **I**, and critical **C** reading questions. (Questions that appear in the student anthology are in regular typeface. Additional questions, which appear only in this teacher's guide, are in italics.)

L What is the first thing that the speaker notices about the filling station?

Answer: It is dirty and "oil-permeated."

I Explain why the speaker says, "Be careful with that match!"

Answer: The speaker is afraid that the oil permeating the station will catch on fire.

L *Describe the father and sons who work and live at the filling station.*

Answer: The father wears oil-soaked overalls; the sons are "quick and saucy and greasy."

I *What is the speaker's attitude toward the father and sons?*

Answer: The speaker disapproves of their dirtiness but is also amused by them. (Other answers are possible.)

I Which items show that someone lives at the filling station?

Answer: the cement porch, wicker furniture, pet dog, comic books, doily, and plant. (Other answers are possible.)

I What details in the poem show that someone loves the filling station—and the people in it?

Answer: Students' answers will vary, but most students will probably agree that the doily and begonia show that someone loves the station and family enough to beautify the surroundings.

I *Who is the "somebody who loves us all" described in the last lines of the poem? Explain your answer.*

Answer: Students' answers will vary, but the begonia and handmade doily will lead many students to believe that the "somebody" is a woman—perhaps the mother of the "greasy sons." (Other answers are possible.)

I *What is the tone of the poem? What details in the poem set the tone?*

Answer: The tone of the poem is light and conversational. This tone is set in the first lines with the exclamations "Oh, but it is dirty!" and "Be careful with that match!" Several other details indicate that the tone is intended to be humorous. In stanza four, the speaker says that "comic books provide the only note . . . of certain color," and in the last stanza, the speaker says, "Somebody waters the plant, / or oils it, maybe."

C *What effect does the poet create through the use of rhetorical questions?*

Answer: The rhetorical questions help to create a conversational tone. The questions invite readers to respond and comment as though the speaker were in a face-to-face conversation with readers.

5. End the lesson with activities that meet students' needs, interests, and learning goals.

· ·

ACTIVITIES

LITERATURE

Setting

1. Point out to students that they will understand the poem better if they visualize where it is set and what the station looks like.

2. Use the following questions to generate discussion:

- In your opinion, where is the filling station located? Along a highway in the country? Along a new tollway? Explain your answers.

- Where are the pumps? Where is the porch?

- What objects are on the porch, and what does each say about life at the filling station?

COMMUNICATION

Self-Perception

1. Ask students which room in their homes is their favorite. Then have students analyze the furnishings and decorations in the room. Ask:

- Which items serve a utilitarian purpose?

- Which items are purely decorative?

- What items would you like to buy for the room? Why?

2. Follow up by asking students to imagine the ideal living room. Tell them that they have unlimited funds with which to buy furniture and decorations for the room. Then ask them to describe how they would furnish and decorate the room so that it expresses their personality.

WRITING

The following assignments may be done in or out of class. **B** designates an assignment suitable for beginning writers; **I**, intermediate writers; **E**, more experienced writers. (Assignments that appear in the student anthology are in regular typeface. Additional assignments, which appear only in this teacher's guide, are in italics.)

B The speaker finds beauty in an unexpected place. Write about a time when you found beauty where you least expected to find it.

I People often personalize an impersonal space by decorating it with items that mean something to them. For example, office workers sometimes decorate their work area with pictures of family members and desk items brought from home. Describe a place that you have "made your own." What items do you keep there? Why are they important to you?

E The speaker says that somebody embroidered the doily, waters the plant, and arranges the rows of oil cans. Who do you think that "somebody" is? What is the person like? Describe the person who gives the filling station tender, loving care.

E *Imagine that you have been invited to go inside the filling-station owners' home. Describe what you think the living room would look like.*

THE LESSON

(PAGES 109-120)

· ·

STORY SUMMARY

Sylvia, a girl from a poor neighborhood in New York City, describes an outing she and her friends take to an expensive toy store in an exclusive area. Miss Moore, who organized the outing, hopes that the contrast in neighborhoods will teach the children to question a "society . . . in which some people . . . spend on a toy what it would cost to feed a family." The lesson is not lost on Sugar, who concludes that "this is not much of a democracy," nor on Sylvia, who vows to "think this day through."

· ·

STEP-BY-STEP LESSON PLAN

1. Ask the pre-reading question:

   - Can you recall what you thought of adults when you were a child? Older children sometimes think that they "know it all" and that adults are hopelessly out of touch with "real life."

To start a discussion, describe an adult that you disliked when you were a child. Ask students if they resented adults who imposed rules on them or tried to teach them "lessons in life."

2. Read the purpose statement aloud to help students set a goal for reading:

   - As you read, think about the title of the story. What lesson is Miss Moore trying to teach Sylvia and the other children?

3. Give students time to read the story silently, or ask them to take turns reading the story aloud.

4. Ask the following literal **L**, interpretive **I**, and critical **C** reading questions. (Questions that appear in the student anthology are in regular typeface. Additional questions, which appear only in this teacher's guide, are in italics.)

L Where do the children live? Describe their neighborhood.

Answer: The children live in apartments in a poor area of New York City frequented by transients.

L *Who is Miss Moore?*

Answer: a college-educated neighborhood woman who wants to give the children the benefits of her education and experience

I How does Sylvia feel about Miss Moore? Why?

Answer: Sylvia resents Miss Moore, perhaps because the woman forces her to confront the realities of the neighborhood in which they live. For example, Sylvia complains that Miss Moore often says they "live in the slums, which I don't feature." (Other answers are possible.)

L What items do the children see in the toy store window? How much does each cost?

Answer: They see a $300 microscope, a $480 paperweight, and a $1,195 sailboat.

I How do Sylvia and Sugar feel when they first enter the toy store?

Answer: awkward, ashamed, and out of place

I Describe the lesson that Miss Moore is trying to teach the children.

Answer: "Poor people have to wake up and demand their share of the pie." (Other answers are possible.)

I Does Sylvia learn the lesson? How do you know?

Answer: Several details indicate that Sylvia has learned the lesson. When Miss Moore discusses the meaning of the trip, Sylvia thinks that "somethin weird is goin on," feels a tightness in her chest, and avoids making eye contact with Miss Moore. Sylvia also shuns Sugar, preferring to "think this day through" alone, and vows that "ain't nobody gonna beat me at nuthin."

C The writer of the story has Sylvia use "bad grammar" and swearwords. Why? Would it improve the story if Sylvia spoke differently? Why or why not?

Answer: Sylvia's manner of speaking reflects the neighborhood in which she lives. Students who disapprove of her speech may believe that the story would be improved if she spoke "standard" English. Other students may believe that Sylvia's speech lends realism and humor to the story.

5. End the lesson with activities that meet students' needs, interests, and learning goals.

· ·

ACTIVITIES

LITERATURE

Characterization

1. Point out that the author develops all of the characters, even the minor ones. On a chalkboard, list the names of all the children. They are as follows:

- Sylvia
- Sugar
- Flyboy
- Fat Butt
- Junebug
- Q.T.
- Rosie Giraffe
- Mercedes

2. Ask students to describe the personality of each child and to support their descriptions with passages from the story.

COMMUNICATION

Sending Messages

1. Point out that the outing begins and ends near a neighborhood mailbox. Ask students why a mailbox is a fitting spot for the characters to meet. Students should see that a mailbox is an appropriate meeting place because Miss Moore has an important message to send to the children.

2. Have students analyze the manner in which the children communicate with each other. Ask:

- Why do the children give each other nicknames?

- Which of the children does not have a nickname? What does the lack of a nickname say about her relationship with the other children?

- Why don't the children give Miss Moore a nickname?

- What does Sylvia mean when she says that Miss Moore is the "only woman on the block with no first name"?

- Why do the children make fun of each other? Does their ridicule stem from dislike or from other motives?

WRITING

The following assignments may be done in or out of class. **B** designates an assignment suitable for beginning writers; **I**, intermediate writers; **E**, more experienced writers. (Assignments that appear in the student anthology are in regular typeface. Additional assignments, which appear only in this teacher's guide, are in italics.)

B Describe a lesson in life that you learned when you were a child.

I The story takes place in two settings—a poor neighborhood and a rich neighborhood. Write about two different neighborhoods in your town or city. Describe what each looks like and how the two neighborhoods are different.

E "The Lesson" is told from Sylvia's point of view. Miss Moore's viewpoint is very different. Imagine that you are Miss Moore. Write a page in your diary or journal about your trip to the toy store. Explain why you took the children, how they reacted, and what you hope they learned.

E *Explain what Miss Moore means by the statement "where you are is who you are." Do you agree with her? Why or why not?*

Contemporary's Whole Language Series

VIEWPOINTS

NONFICTION SELECTIONS

GREAT MOMENTS

(PAGES 3-17)

· ·

THEME SUMMARY

The three people in the readings faced serious obstacles. They also shared a common goal of wanting to express themselves. Elizabeth Cotten overcame poverty and discrimination and became a well-known musician. Helen Keller, unable to hear, see, or speak, learned sign language. Christy Brown, paralyzed by cerebral palsy, learned to use his left foot to write. Each person became an inspiration to others. (Note: "Andrew" and "Tickits," in *Expressions*, would make good companion pieces to these selections.)

· ·

STEP-BY-STEP LESSON PLAN

1. Ask the pre-reading questions:

   • Have you ever felt defeated and that everything and everyone was against you? Have you felt that you could be happier if there weren't so many roadblocks between you and a goal?

   Start a discussion by giving examples of people you have known who have overcome obstacles or roadblocks. You might want to discuss the backgrounds of the people in the three readings.

2. Read the purpose statement aloud to help students set a goal for reading:

   • As you read, think about what roadblock each person had to overcome in order to achieve success.

3. Give students time to read each piece silently. Or you might want to read the first one aloud, review the purpose statement, and then assign the other readings.

4. Ask students to summarize the main idea of each reading. Then ask the following literal **L**, interpretive **I**, and critical **C** reading questions. (Questions that appear in the student anthology are in regular typeface. Additional questions, which appear only in this teacher's guide, are in italics.)

L What roadblock did Elizabeth Cotten, Helen Keller, and Christy Brown each overcome? How did each person's life change as a result of overcoming the roadblock?

Answer: Elizabeth Cotten was disadvantaged—she lived in poverty and in a segregated society—yet she developed her own style of guitar playing and received a Grammy award. Helen Keller could not hear, see, or speak after a childhood illness, but she learned to communicate with sign language. Christy Brown couldn't speak or control the use of his body due to cerebral palsy; he learned how to use his left foot to write.

I Which two people's stories are similar? Why?

Answer: Helen Keller and Christy Brown were both disabled and unable to speak. Each discovered a new means of communicating—through touching.

L Explain how all three people shared the same goal of wanting to communicate with others.

Answer: Elizabeth Cotten—to tell her story through song and by playing guitar; Helen Keller—to communicate in spite of not being able to see, hear, or talk; Christy Brown—to write even though he couldn't control his arms or legs.

L Each of the three people had the support of another person. Tell who helped each one.

Answer: Elizabeth Cotten—her mother; Helen Keller—her teacher; Christy Brown—his mother.

I Which details show that Elizabeth Cotten's childhood was disadvantaged?

Answer: Her parents didn't give her a first name; her family had to hide their meat so white people wouldn't take it from them; she made 75 cents a month as a housekeeper.

L *How did Helen Keller's attitude toward Anne Sullivan change?*

Answer: Her feelings changed from rage to curiosity when she realized she could learn the meanings of words from her teacher.

L *Did Christy Brown realize the importance of being able to use his left foot to write? How do you know?*

Answer: Yes; he shared his excitement and frustration at the moment he chose to try to use the yellow chalk. He called learning to write the letter *A* "my road to a new world, my key to mental freedom."

C *Each reading tells about what happened to the person as a child. Why does each author first focus on what happened to the person as a child?*

Answer: Each story focuses on obstacles that had to be overcome early in the person's life before he or she could achieve success.

5. End the lesson with activities that meet students' needs, interests, and learning goals.

. . . .

ACTIVITIES

RHETORIC

Characterization: Comparison and Contrast

1. Write each of the three people's names on the board. List with students the characteristics of each person.

   - Identify their similarities (need to communicate; isolation from others; events in childhood).

   - Then identify their differences (Elizabeth Cotten was not physically disabled; Helen Keller was not poor; Christy Brown wrote a letter while Helen Keller used signing).

2. Look at each selection's conclusion. Ask students:

   - How does the ending of each reading tell us more about each character?

Language and Style

Discuss the difference between an interview (Elizabeth Cotten), a biography (Helen Keller), and an autobiography (Christy Brown).

1. Ask students to identify who told each story.

   - Ask which they prefer—*first-person narration* (a story told in a person's own words) or *third-person* (a story told from another person's point of view).

2. Review each author's language and style. Ask the following:

   - Elizabeth Cotten was interviewed. What are some examples in which the interviewer used Elizabeth's own words?

   - How did Catherine Peare show the readers that Helen Keller was using "finger tricks" to spell out each word?

   - Christy Brown couldn't speak or write as a child, but he could hear and touch. What did he feel and hear as he tried to write the letter *A*?

COMMUNICATION

Nonverbal Clues

Helen Keller and Christy Brown both communicated nonverbally. Elizabeth Cotten could not read music; she used her sense of hearing to make music. Ask students:

1. If you were Helen Keller, which sense would you rely on the most? Why?

2. What nonverbal clues did Christy Brown's family give as he tried to write with the yellow chalk for the first time?

Perception

Discuss with students the importance of having positive attitudes toward people with disabilities.

1. Invite one of the following people to class: someone who can demonstrate sign language, someone who can show materials written in braille, or someone who can demonstrate "Cotten pickin'."

2. Ask students to name some disabled people who have been cast in TV or movie roles.

WRITING

The following assignments may be done in or out of class. **B** designates an assignment suitable for beginning writers; **I**, intermediate writers; **E**, more experienced writers. (Assignments that appear in the student anthology are in regular typeface. Additional assignments, which appear only in this teacher's guide, are in italics.)

B Is there a roadblock that is stopping you from reaching one of your goals? Write a paragraph describing how you might overcome the roadblock.

I Which of the three people in the readings do you most admire? Why? Write a letter to the person explaining your views.

E Do you know someone who has had a "great moment" like the ones these three people experienced? Describe the person and what happened because of that moment.

E *Each of the three people in the readings achieved something he or she was proud of. Describe a personal achievement that you take pride in.*

For more information, look for the following at your local library: *The Miracle Worker* (video, play, or book); *My Left Foot* (video or book); *Elizabeth Cotten Live* (album or tape).

FAMILY RELATIONSHIPS

(PAGES 19-35)

. . . .

THEME SUMMARY

These readings are about relationships between parents and children and show examples of strong family support—receiving it as children and passing it on as adults. A young athlete, Mark Messner, shows an unselfish devotion to his dying stepfather. Billie Jean Young and Nolan Ryan both express appreciation for the family support they got when they were young and that enabled them to become successful adults.

. . . .

STEP-BY-STEP LESSON PLAN

1. Ask the pre-reading questions:

   • As a child, were you raised in a traditional family, with a mother, father, brothers, and sisters? Or were you raised by a stepmother, a grandparent, an aunt, or someone not a blood relative?

Start a discussion by giving examples of your own family background. Encourage students to share the differences and similarities in their family backgrounds.

2. Read the purpose statement aloud to help students set a goal for reading:

   • As you read, think about your relationships with the members of your family.

3. Give students time to read each piece silently. Or you might want to read the first one aloud, review the purpose statement, and then assign the other readings.

4. Ask students to summarize the main idea of each reading. Then ask the following literal **L**, interpretive **I**, and critical **C** reading questions. (Questions that appear in the student anthology are in regular typeface. Additional questions, which appear only in this teacher's guide, are in italics.)

I How does Mark Messner become "father to the man" in his relationship with Del Pretty? Are the roles between parents and children sometimes reversed? Explain how this might happen.

Answer: Mark Messner takes on the role of father to his dying stepfather, Del Pretty. Mark Messner's devotion comes out of the love his stepfather gave to him throughout his life. Yes—as parents age and become ill, children are often responsible for the care of their parents.

L How did Billie Jean Young's mother help give her a second chance? Do you know a mother and daughter with a similar relationship?

Answer: Billie Jean Young's mother took care of her (Billie Jean's) boys so that Billie could finish her education and work part-time. Answers to the second part of the question will vary.

C Which writer examines the traditional family structure? Which two writers show nontraditional family structures? Explain.

Answer: Nolan Ryan writes about a married couple and their children. Billie Jean Young and Mitch Albom write about relationships with single parents.

L What personal goal does Nolan Ryan have as a father concerning his children?

Answer: He wants to raise his kids in the same kind of atmosphere that he grew up in—caring for and loving each other.

L *Besides family support, we rely on community support. How did Billie Jean Young's community let her down when she was a teen?*

Answer: Her church rejected her; at school she was poorly treated; she could not get a job in her town.

I *Many parents tell their children, "You'll understand when you have children of your own." How does this statement apply to both Billie Jean Young and her mother?*

Answer: Billie Jean Young's mother had been alone with children and had gone to her parents for help, so she understood when Billie needed her help raising children. Billie now understood how Mama must have felt as a grandmother.

5. End the lesson with activities that meet students' needs, interests, and learning goals.

··

ACTIVITIES

RHETORIC

Organization

Review methods of organization that writers use (chronological order, cause and effect, comparison and contrast). Ask students to identify some patterns of organization used in the readings. Sample patterns used by Mitch Albom in "Mark Messner" include:

> chronological order—progression of Del Pretty's illness; cause and effect—effects of chemotherapy on Del Pretty; comparison and contrast—mention of photo showing how Del Pretty looked before and after his illness

Language and Style

Each of the three readings presents a different style of writing. Ask students to identify elements of style used by Mitch Albom. Suggested ideas include:

- repetition of "Isn't life funny?," emotional conclusion, use of dialogue, use of flashback

COMMUNICATION

Nonverbal Behavior

1. Identify the ways some of the people in the readings showed their love for family members (Mark Messner—feeds and bathes his dying stepfather; Billie Jean Young—passes on her mother's legacy of love to her own grandchildren; Nolan Ryan—raises his kids in a loving atmosphere).

2. Ask students to discuss things they *do* for their families that send the message "I love you."

3. Have students explain the traditions unique to their families.

Perception

Write on the board the word *family*. Work as a group to write a definition.

Raise questions such as:

- Is a childless couple a family?

- Can two males or two females raising children be considered a family?

- When is *family* a legal term? (building ordinances)

- What's the difference between a family and a household?

···

WRITING

The following assignments may be done in or out of class. **B** designates an assignment suitable for beginning writers; **I**, intermediate writers; **E**, more experienced writers. (Assignments that appear in the student anthology are in regular typeface. Additional assignments, which appear only in this teacher's guide, are in italics.)

B Mark Messner thought of Del Pretty as his father. Describe someone who is not related by blood but is like family to you.

I Nolan Ryan vividly remembers the day the Little League announcer predicted Ryan's success in the major leagues. Write a journal entry about a childhood activity that affected your life's direction.

I *Mitch Albom tells us: "count your blessings. . . . One precious person at a time." Is there anyone you consider a blessing in your life? Write a letter telling that person why you consider him or her a blessing.*

E Is there anything unique about your family? Write a paragraph explaining what makes it special.

E *Has someone close to you ever become seriously ill or died? Describe how this experience affected your life.*

E *These are the last words of a poem Del Pretty wrote, which Mark Messner read at his stepfather's funeral: "If all else in a man's life added to zero, no greater success than to be counted his son's hero." Do you agree with this statement? Explain why or why not.*

PRIDE IN WORK

(PAGES 37-53)

· ·

THEME SUMMARY

The first reading is a personal narrative by Carol Hazel, a mother of four, who learned skills for a new job and was able to lift herself up. The second reading is an interview with Eddie Lovett, a self-taught man, who reads every day in order to better educate himself and his children. The third reading is about Lucy Lim, a Chinese-Mexican-American woman who, influenced by her father, was taught to work hard. She has succeeded in jobs previously closed to minority women. Each person has gained confidence and freedom through hard work and feels the effort has been worth it.

· ·

STEP-BY-STEP LESSON PLAN

1. Ask the pre-reading questions:

   • Are you happy in your work? Do you look forward to going to work or to the way you spend each day?

Start a discussion by giving examples of people you know who love their work and are proud of their accomplishments.

2. Read the purpose statement to help students set a goal for reading:

   • As you read, think about why each person works so hard and feels good about himself or herself.

3. Give students time to read each piece silently. Or you might want to read the first one aloud, review the purpose statement, and then assign the other readings.

4. Ask students to summarize the main idea of each reading. Then ask the following literal **L**, interpretive **I**, and critical **C** reading questions. (Questions that appear in the student anthology are in regular typeface. Additional questions, which appear only in this teacher's guide, are in italics.)

L How does each person feel about his or her work? Give details from each reading.

Answer: Carol Hazel talks about her need to be known. She doesn't want money she didn't have the chance to earn. Eddie Lovett likes to ponder in his library and has declared war upon his ignorance. Lucy Lim really enjoys her job. She never knows what will be in store for her when she arrives at work.

I How are the two women's jobs similar?

Answer: Both work in nontraditional jobs for women; both wear hard hats and do physical labor; both learned new skills to enter new job areas.

I Carol Hazel says, "And I'm raising my children well, lifting myself up. . . ." Explain how each of the three people has lifted himself or herself up.

Answer: Carol Hazel got off welfare, went to school, and got a job she liked. Eddie Lovett learned how to read and passed on his love of learning to his children. Lucy Lim got a college degree and found a nontraditional job that pays well and that she enjoys.

I Do you know anyone who shares Eddie Lovett's love of reading and learning? Explain.

Answer: Answers will vary; use as class discussion.

L How has Lucy Lim's family background influenced her sense of self?

Answer: She has a Chinese father and a Mexican mother and so has a varied cultural background. Her father taught her independence and the importance of working hard. Her brother never treated her differently because she was female.

I How are other people benefiting from the work done by each of the three people?

Answer: Eddie Lovett's children have learned to love reading as much as he does. Lucy Lim has helped to break down employment barriers for women and minorities. Carol Hazel will be able to tell her grandchildren with pride, "That's my stone."

C Two of the readings are told from a personal point of view. The other reading is an interview. Which form of writing do you think works better? Why?

Answer: Answers will vary; use as class discussion.

I *What skills do you take pride in? Why?*

Answer: Answers will vary.

5. End the lesson with activities that meet students' needs, interests, and learning goals.

ACTIVITIES

RHETORIC

Characterization: Compare and Contrast

1. Write the three people's names on the board.

   - Identify with students the similarities in how the three people feel about their jobs (the obstacles they have overcome, the importance of families, their sense of purpose, their views of the future).

   - Then identify the differences (Eddie does not get paid for his work; the women do physical labor while Eddie's work is intellectual).

2. List on the board two headings: *Male* and *Female*. Under each heading, write two subheadings: *traditional jobs* and *nontraditional jobs*. Then ask students to place jobs under these categories. (Example: *Male traditional* or *female nontraditional*—construction worker, manager; *male nontraditional* or *female traditional*—nurse, secretary.)

Language and Style

1. Discuss with students the fact that in an interview, the writer uses the exact words of the person he or she is interviewing, including the person's regional dialect.

2. Look at the readings about Eddie Lovett and Lucy Lim for examples of the type of language used by each person.

   - Eddie Lovett—informal style of speech and his regional dialect, characterized by adding an *s* to present verb tenses

   - Lucy Lim—technical terms she uses to explain what she does on her job

COMMUNICATION

Talking to Ourselves

1. Discuss with students the idea that what we think, feel, or believe about ourselves or what we can do affects what we can accomplish in our lives.

   - Note the positive message Carol Hazel gave herself about cutting stone when she said, *"I can do that."*

   - Think about the messages we give ourselves and whether they are positive or negative: "I'll keep trying until I get it right" (positive); "I'm a slow learner" (negative).

2. Brainstorm for other messages we give ourselves and list them on the board. Then discuss whether they have a negative or positive effect.

Perception

Ask students to think of ways in which they are improving their lives—by taking classes, learning new skills, striving for better jobs, and so on.

1. Invite each student to interview another student in class.

2. As a group, develop five or six questions to ask another student. (How do you feel about your job? Why do or don't you like it? What obstacles have you overcome? What new skills are you learning in school? What job would you like to have?)

3. After the interview, each student should be given an opportunity to share what he or she has learned about the other person.

WRITING

The following assignments may be done in or out of class. **B** designates an assignment suitable for beginning writers; **I**, intermediate writers; **E**, more experienced writers. (Assignments that appear in the student anthology are in regular typeface. Additional assignments, which appear only in this teacher's guide, are in italics.)

B Are you happy in your work? Why or why not? Write a journal entry explaining how you feel about a typical work day.

I Who is the hardest-working person you know? In a paragraph, describe the person and why he or she is motivated to work so hard.

I Do you know someone who, like Carol Hazel, has lifted herself—or himself—up? How did the person overcome obstacles or make changes in his or her life? Write a letter to the person explaining how you feel about the accomplishments.

I *What is your dream job? Describe it.*

E All three people learned new skills as they worked to improve their lives. As a result, each person gained personal freedom. Do you agree that education is the key to freedom? Write a few paragraphs describing how education has affected your life.

NO PLACE LIKE HOME
(PAGES 55-71)

· ·

THEME SUMMARY

Each reading presents a man, woman, child, or family who has somehow become homeless. While little Shizuye Takashima has shelter, she has been relocated by the government. Not knowing whether she is Japanese or Canadian represents her conflict in not knowing where her "home" is. Similarly, when the U.S. government took over Indian lands, it was rejecting who the Indians were as well as restricting where they were allowed to live. And Bob Greene's and Jonathan Kozol's examples are about some of our current homeless population. All four readings are about the desire to have a place of our own, a home.

· ·

STEP-BY-STEP LESSON PLAN

1. Ask the pre-reading questions:

   • What does *home* mean to you? Is it where you live now? Do you still live in the area where you grew up, or have you moved several times during your life?

Start a discussion by giving your own answer to the questions. Share how you feel about your home.

2. Read the purpose statements aloud to help students set a goal for reading:

   • As you read, think about what you would do if you no longer had your home or apartment, or any place to live. Think about what you would do if you lost your job, or if your home was destroyed by fire, or taken away from you because of urban renewal.

3. Give students time to read each piece silently. Or you might want to read the first one aloud, review the purpose statements, and then assign the other readings.

4. Ask students to summarize the main idea of each reading. Then ask the following literal **L**, interpretive **I**, and critical **C** reading questions. (Questions that appear in the student anthology are in regular typeface. Additional questions, which appear only in this teacher's guide, are in italics.)

I Did David Gambill do the right thing by calling the police when he found the man in his home? What would you have done in his situation?

Answer: Answers will vary; use for class discussion.

L What reasons does Celsa Apapas, the Cupeño Indian woman, give for not wanting to leave her home?

Answer: Her ancestors are buried there. She believes the mountains belong to her, and God gave her people their home. To her, home is where you are born and where you die.

I In "Spring 1944," Shizuye Takashima says, "Really, maybe children should rule the world!" What causes her to make this statement?

Answer: She feels tired, confused, and helpless. She calls the war senseless. (Other answers are possible.)

I Which of the readings do you find the saddest? Why?

Answer: Answers will vary. Remind students that these are nonfiction (real-life situations), not fiction (short stories).

C Why do you think Jonathan Kozol called his introduction "Ordinary People"? How are Peter, Megan, and their children ordinary?

Answer: A tragedy such as a fire can happen to anyone. This ordinary family became instantly homeless. When parents lose their jobs, they no longer have the money to pay for rent, food, or clothes, and they can become homeless. (Other answers are possible.)

L Was Shizuye Takashima Japanese or Canadian? Explain your answer.

Answer: Her family is of Oriental descent, so they look Japanese because their father was born in Japan. However, the children were born in Canada. Today, they might be called Japanese Canadian (such as French Canadian, Mexican American, African American).

C What is Bob Greene's purpose in writing "Stranger at the Table"? Which do you think is more effective—a story showing an example, or an essay giving facts and opinions?

Answer: Bob Greene is teaching by example instead of editorializing. (Students may discuss which type of nonfiction they prefer.)

L *When Jonathan Kozol sees Peter and Megan two years later, how have their lives changed? Why?*

Answer: They have turned to begging for money. Because they could not provide for the children, Peter and Megan had to give them up for adoption.

5. End the lesson with activities that meet students' needs, interests, and learning goals.

ACTIVITIES

RHETORIC

Characterization: Contrasts

1. Ask students to identify the differences between David Gambill and Allen Young.

   - What is each man's lifestyle? (Allen Young has to steal food to survive; David Gambill is returning from vacation and owns a nice family home.)

   - Who is the victim, or are both? (David Gambill is a victim of a crime; Allen Young is a victim of society.)

   - Who shows more emotion? (David Gambill is bothered more by the incident because nothing like that has ever happened to him before.)

   - Who is more in control of the situation? (Allen Young suggests calling the police instead of trying to escape.)

2. Discuss the situations of the people in each of the other readings.

   - Why are Peter and Megan's children and Takashima not in control of their lives?

   - Point out the role of the U.S. government in some of the cases: the Japanese-American families during World War II; Native Americans; Peter and Megan's losing their children.

Language and Style

Two of the readings are written in unusual styles. Ask students to find examples from the texts.

1. "Spring 1944"

   - the use of a child's view of adults

   - the use of short lines retelling the author's memories of the camp

2. "Ordinary People"

   - excerpt is an introduction to a book about homelessness

   - Jonathan Kozol writes observations and facts and not opinions.

COMMUNICATION

Problem Solving

1. Divide the class into pairs or groups.

2. Brainstorm together for a list of reasons why some people are homeless. Explain cause-and-effect, or chain-of-events, organization.

   - fire or eviction, no place to go, no education or skills, no job, no money, no food, illness

3. Ask for solutions to some of the problems listed.

   - Differentiate between "Whose fault is it?," "Whose responsibility is it?," and "How are we going to end homelessness?" (Examples of solutions are low-cost apartments or working for rent.)

Perception

1. Ask students: Does your community have a homeless shelter or program?

   - Suggest ways to research: calling the local United Way, hospital, police station, or clergy.

2. Provide information about local programs.

   - Suggest a project such as a canned-food collection.

WRITING

The following assignments may be done in or out of class. **B** designates an assignment suitable for beginning writers; **I**, intermediate writers; **E**, more experienced writers. (Assignments that appear in the student anthology are in regular typeface. Additional assignments, which appear only in this teacher's guide, are in italics.)

B Do you know people who have lost their homes? Explain what happened and how they coped.

I Jonathan Kozol writes about people who were "up some" but who are now "down and out." Do you know anyone who, for some reason, was down and out but who survived and is living better now?

I Shizuye Takashima's father states to her mother, "Never mind the children. . . . They'll adjust." Do you agree that children adjust easily to a new home or to other changes? Give examples.

E Have you ever been approached by someone begging for money to buy food? Write a journal entry with details of what happened when you were approached and how you reacted and felt.

E *Make a list of questions you would like to ask someone who works with the homeless. Then use your list to interview a volunteer at a community center. Present the results in a report written in a question-and-answer format.*

TIME OUT TO LAUGH
(PAGES 73-85)

....

THEME SUMMARY

These three readings look at everyday situations in a humorous way. Shirley Jackson relates the way each of her children reacts to a new baby brother in the family. Andy Rooney contrasts how his Saturday would be if he had help from the White House staff with what his day is really like. Bill Cosby reflects on the ways his children are growing up and away from him, especially his college-age daughter.

....

STEP-BY-STEP LESSON PLAN

1. Ask the pre-reading question:

   • Do you sometimes take life too seriously, or do you have a good sense of humor even when things are not going well?

Start a discussion by asking students if they have heard expressions such as "Stop and smell the roses." Ask for examples from their daily lives that suggest that life is so busy they don't take time to relax.

2. Read the purpose statement aloud to help students set a goal for reading:

   • As you read, think about your need to take time out to laugh once in a while.

3. Give students time to read each piece silently. Or you might want to read the first one aloud, review the purpose statement, and then assign the other readings.

4. Ask students to summarize the main idea of each reading. Then ask the following literal **L**, interpretive **I**, and critical **C** reading questions. (Questions that appear in the student anthology are in regular typeface. Additional questions, which appear only in this teacher's guide, are in italics.)

L How does each of Shirley Jackson's children react to the new baby?

Answer: Sally is too young to understand where the baby came from; Jannie and Laurie think the baby is too small; Laurie is quickly bored by the event.

I Like many parents, Jackson and her husband are a little nervous about bringing home a new baby. Why?

Answer: Most parents are not sure how brothers and sisters will accept the new family member.

L How is Andy Rooney's Saturday morning made easier when he receives imaginary help from the White House staff?

Answer: He is served breakfast in bed and given help with dressing, summarizing news, sorting mail, paying bills, making repairs, and getting his hair cut.

L What parts of Bill Cosby's piece are funny? What parts are serious?

Answer: Answers will vary; use as class discussion.

L How does Jackson humorously describe each of her children when she sees them standing on the porch?

Answer: Jannie's hair is uncombed; she has on a sundress and is barefoot. Laurie needs a haircut; he is wearing a pair of sneakers he took out of the garbage can. Sally has chocolate all over her face; she is wearing Laurie's fur hat.

C Shirley Jackson does not explain what *it* is immediately. Why do you think she does this?

Answer: Jackson is building suspense in her story and making it more interesting.

C *Bill Cosby says, "We cannot make a part-time commitment to our children. . . . We have to stay tuned in to them." Do you think it's possible to do this, given the busy pace of our daily lives? Why or why not?*

Answer: Answers will vary; use as class discussion.

I *If you have something serious to tell someone, do you ever try to make a joke about it? Give an example.*

Answer: Answers will vary; use as class discussion.

5. End the lesson with activities that meet students' needs, interests, and learning goals.

....

ACTIVITIES

RHETORIC

Organization: Supporting Ideas

1. Point out that Andy Rooney uses lists in his essay.

   • Ask students to give examples of lists from the essay.

2. Discuss how Jackson shows that Laurie is the oldest child, Jannie the second, and Sally the youngest . . . until the baby comes. What does each child react to that shows his or her birth order?

3. Read aloud the ending of one of the essays.

   • Show how a strong ending ties together the theme and supports the ideas presented in the essay.

Language and Style: Humor

1. All three writers use humor in their essays.

   • Find examples from Andy Rooney showing the humor in a *situation.* ("Followed by four Secret Service operatives, I drive to the car wash, where they see to it that I go to the head of the line.")

   • Note how Bill Cosby and Shirley Jackson both inject humor about a *person.* (Cosby talks about his young son as a "wee airborne terror," and if you are going on a trip with him, "make sure that you travel in separate planes." Jackson's children refer to their new brother as "it" instead of "him." They think the baby is too small and wonder if it's the best their parents could get.)

COMMUNICATION

Sharing Stories

1. Ask students to tell a story about something they believed as a child, such as "where babies come from." Invite students to share stories about their inaccurate beliefs.

2. Then ask students to tell about times when they laughed with their families or friends and what caused their laughter.

Perception

Humor can be used in a positive or a negative way. Ask students to think about instances when they experienced each type of humor.

1. Recall situations in which humor was used appropriately. Some examples might be:

   • a film that had truly entertaining moments

   • a speaker who told a joke to relax the audience

   • a comedian who made people laugh at life's funny events

2. Then discuss situations in which humor was used inappropriately to laugh at people. Some examples might be:

   • when a person made a mistake in speech or behavior

   • when a person looked different from "normal" people

   • when a person's racial or ethnic background was laughed at

3. End the discussion by asking students which instances made them feel comfortable and which made them feel uncomfortable.

WRITING

The following assignments may be done in or out of class. **B** designates an assignment suitable for beginning writers; **I**, intermediate writers; **E**, more experienced writers. (Assignments that appear in the student anthology are in regular typeface. Additional assignments, which appear only in this teacher's guide, are in italics.)

B Imagine that the White House staff will help you for one morning. Contrast a typical day with the kind of day you could have with their help.

I Do you think parents today worry too much or worry too little about their children? Choose one view and give examples.

I *Is there someone in your family that you consider to be funny? Write a humorous description.*

E Bill Cosby talks about how quickly our children grow up and move away from us. Given the lack of time, what values do you think parents should pass on to their children before the children move away?

E Imagine that you are a child meeting a new baby brother or sister for the first time. Write a journal entry telling how you feel. What would you say to your parents about the baby?

E Do you agree with Bill Cosby's statement that "we all make mistakes with our kids, but we can learn from them [mistakes] and grow with them [kids]"? Explain your views in a paragraph.

VOICES FROM THE PAST

(PAGES 87-97)

· ·

THEME SUMMARY

All three readings acknowledge a change in a way of life. Black Hawk admits defeat and is forced to accept the victory of the white man and the eventual end of the Indian way of life. Everette Tharp speaks of a changing world where progress in the form of a railroad ended the era of the mountain people. Martin Luther King, Jr., calls for changes that will bring justice and equal rights to black Americans. Change is not always progress. We seem to lose while we gain. Whatever happens, if we listen to the voices from the past, we can better appreciate what we need for our future. (Note: "Montgomery," in *Expressions*, would make a good companion piece to these selections.)

· ·

STEP-BY-STEP LESSON PLAN

1. Ask the pre-reading questions:

   • Have you ever wished you had lived in another time and place in history? What changes might you have taken part in if you had lived during an earlier time?

Start a discussion by giving examples of favorite eras. Review times when clothes were more interesting or when customs or events seemed more exciting.

2. Read the purpose statement aloud to help sudents set a goal for reading:

   • As you read, think about the changing world that each writer or speaker faces. Think about what each person lost and gained.

3. Give students time to read each piece silently. Or you might want to read the first one aloud, review the purpose statement, and then assign the other readings.

4. Ask students to summarize the main idea of each reading. Then ask the following literal **L**, interpretive **I**, and critical **C** reading questions. (Questions that appear in the student anthology are in regular typeface. Additional questions, which appear only in this teacher's guide, are in italics.)

L Which two readings tell of a loss of harmony with nature, an end to living off the land?

Answer: Everette Tharp describes a changing Appalachia, and Black Hawk fights the white man's stealing of his land.

I What makes a good leader? Were Chief Black Hawk and Martin Luther King, Jr., both good leaders? Give a reason for your opinion.

Answer: A good leader inspires others to do things. Both men had followers who believed in them and who were willing to die for them. (Other answers are possible.)

I Describe what you think life was like in Appalachia in the early 1900s, given the absence of radios, TVs, cars, railroads, and airplanes.

Answer: It was a much slower, simpler way of life. People depended on the land for survival. They enjoyed the beauty of nature. They may have been satisfied with much less than we are today. (Other answers are possible.)

I Which of these voices from the past did you find most interesting? Why?

Answer: Answers will vary; use as class discussion.

C "Farewell to Black Hawk" is written by Black Hawk in the first person, using "I" at the beginning, and then changes to the third person, using "he." Why do you think he wrote his speech in this way?

Answer: Black Hawk is speaking about his determination to fight the white man and not be defeated by him. After he is taken prisoner, Black Hawk feels dead, so he speaks about himself as if he is speaking about another person.

I How do you think Black Hawk and Everette Tharp would feel about the environment today?

Answer: Black Hawk would feel he was right about the white man's way of life—it has destroyed what Indians considered sacred. Tharp might not be surprised; she viewed the railroad as the beginning of the end for the natural surroundings.

I *In your opinion, has Dr. King's dream come true? Why do you feel as you do?*

Answer: Students' answers will vary.

5. End the lesson with activities that meet students' needs, interests, and learning goals.

···

ACTIVITIES

RHETORIC

Characterization

Ask students to consider the viewpoint of Everette Tharp.

- Everette Tharp (born in 1899) describes her lifestyle of rural simplicity. Was it a better way of life back then? What do you think a woman's life was like in the mountains?

Language and Style

1. Choose one of the speeches (King's or Black Hawk's) and ask a student to read it aloud.

   - You might also check a library for a recording of King's speech so that students can hear his intonation.

2. Ask students to identify the following:

   From Martin Luther King's speech:

   - his repetition of words and phrases ("I have a dream"; "Let freedom ring")

   - his use of quotations from other sources (the Bible and songs)

   From Black Hawk's speech:

   - his use of first person ("I") and then third person ("he")

   - his contrasts of the Indian with the white man

   - his use of vivid images, comparisons (the sun to a ball of fire, and of the white man to a snake), and *alliteration* (repetition of beginning sounds—"The *b*ullets flew like *b*irds in the air, and *wh*izzed by our heads like the *w*ind through the trees in *w*inter").

COMMUNICATION

Visual Messages

Suggest to students that history can be recorded by methods other than writing (for example: paintings, photography, architecture, and other art).

1. Bring in a few photographs, posters, or other works that represent the main ideas of each reading. Ask students how the art portrays each topic:

- Appalachia—mountain men and women or rural way of life

- the civil rights struggle—segregation, integration, or protests

- Native American culture—famous chiefs, artifacts, or reservations

2. Follow up by asking students to look for more examples of art and to explain what message they think each piece conveys.

Perception

1. Ask students to identify the most significant historical event during their lives.

   - What story will they tell their grandchildren?

2. Then ask some students to tell or read their story to the class.

WRITING

The following assignments may be done in or out of class. **B** designates an assignment suitable for beginning writers; **I**, intermediate writers; **E**, more experienced writers. (Assignments that appear in the student anthology are in regular typeface. Additional assignments, which appear only in this teacher's guide, are in italics.)

B Have you ever known an elderly person who talked about the past and the changes he or she has seen? Write a paragraph briefly describing the oral history you were told.

B *Would you like to live in Everette Tharp's "old Appalachia"—without TVs, radios, stereos, or CD players? Why or why not?*

I Write a short speech. Use the "I Have a Dream" speech as a model. List four or five of your hopes for the future. Begin each paragraph with "I have a dream that. . . ."

E In 1963, Martin Luther King, Jr., hoped that all people in America would one day be treated equally. Do you think we are getting closer today to equality for all people? Write a few paragraphs supporting your opinion.

E Imagine that you are a columnist. Choose one way you see our world changing (environment, laws and rules, car or house designs, fashion, lifestyles). Write a few paragraphs expressing your opinion for a column that might appear in your local newspaper.

REALIZING DREAMS

(PAGES 99-109)

. . . .

THEME SUMMARY

"Realizing Dreams" is about individuals who had dreams and, in order to reach those dreams, set goals and completed tasks toward an end. Larry Walters wanted to fly in his lawn chair; Simon Rodia wanted to build beautiful towers. Each developed his own method and saw it through with determination. Janice Payan realized her dream of becoming successful and shared her story with other Hispanic women. All three people believe that anything is possible if you try hard enough.

. . . .

STEP-BY-STEP LESSON PLAN

1. Ask the pre-reading question:

   • Do you believe that you have the ability to do anything you want to do in life?

Start a discussion by giving examples of your dreams, past and present. Discuss with students the difference between a wish, a fantasy, a dream, and a goal. Encourage students to share stories about people they know who worked hard for their dreams.

2. Read the purpose statement aloud to help students set a goal for reading:

   • As you read, think about your dreams—ones you have had in the past and ones you still have now. What do you hope will happen to you and to the world during your lifetime?

3. Give students time to read each piece silently. Or you might want to read the first one aloud, review the purpose statement and question, and then assign the other readings.

4. Ask students to summarize the main idea of each reading. Then ask the following literal **L**, interpretive **I**, and critical **C** reading questions. (Questions that appear in the student anthology are in regular typeface. Additional questions, which appear only in this teacher's guide, are in italics.)

I Robert Fulghum writes, "The human race sits in its chair." What should we be doing instead?

Answer: We should use our imaginations, have dreams, and know that anything is possible. (Other answers are possible.)

I Which type of person are you, a doubter or a dreamer? Are you content to sit in a chair, or would you rather try to fly in it?

Answer: Answers will vary; use as class discussion.

L How are Simon Rodia and Larry Walters alike?

Answer: Both men had dreams that they worked on until they became real. Rodia wanted to build towers; Walters wanted to fly in a lawn chair.

L According to Janice Payan, what barriers do Hispanic women face?

Answer: They must overcome racism, sexism, and poverty.

I Janice Payan is now a successful executive and is living her dream. What was the most important step toward realizing her achievements?

Answer: education; attending college

C *Look at the title of the book about Simon Rodia. Do you think it is a good title? Explain.*

Answer: *Beautiful Junk* seems to be a good title. Simon Rodia spent over thirty years collecting junk (pieces of tile, glass, metal, and so on) to create his beautiful towers.

I *Janice Payan set her goals on "having a marriage, a family, and a career." Do you think it is more possible for a woman to realize all three goals today than it was in the past? Explain.*

Answer: Answers will vary; use as class discussion.

5. End the lesson with activities that meet students' needs, interests, and learning goals.

. . . .

ACTIVITIES

RHETORIC

Characterization: Compare and Contrast

1. List the names of Larry Walters and Simon Rodia on the board.

2. Ask students to identify under each name:

   • the dream

- the length of time spent in reaching his goal

- the method of reaching his goal

- his reaction to reaching the dream

Language and Style

1. Analyze Janice Payan's speech, "It's Up to Us." The speech is meant to inspire women. Find support for each of these:

   - examples of how she is like the women she is speaking to (her cultural and economic background; her struggle to make her dreams come true)

   - examples of humor ("If I'm so smart, why can't I parallel park?"; "I was raised with typical Hispanic female expectations. In other words: If you want to *do* well in life, you'd better . . . can anybody finish that sentence? Right! *Marry well.*")

   - examples that show she is interacting with her audience (asking them to raise their hands; answering "right")

2. Ask: "Why does she list names of other Hispanic women?" (to cite role models—other Hispanic women who rose from humble beginnings and achieved their dreams).

3. Then follow up by discussing why we need role models.

COMMUNICATION

Goal Setting

Larry Walters had a plan. His dream was to fly, so he spent time preparing to achieve his dream.

1. Ask students to work alone or in pairs to develop some personal goals.

2. Each student should write one goal under each of these headings:

   - tomorrow

   - within a week

   - within a month

   - within a year

   - within five years

3. Have students discuss with a partner exactly how they will accomplish each goal. How are the goals related to a dream?

Perception

1. Work as a group to develop a list of people (performers, sports figures, heroes) who have recently achieved their dreams.

2. Ask students to explain how they feel when they see others' successes:

   - Super Bowl, World Series

   - Academy awards, Grammy awards

   - relative's graduation or retirement

3. Bring in or ask students to find news articles or feature stories about people achieving goals and fulfilling dreams.

WRITING

The following assignments may be done in or out of class. **B** designates an assignment suitable for beginning writers; **I**, intermediate writers; **E**, more experienced writers. (Assignments that appear in the student anthology are in regular typeface. Additional assignments, which appear only in this teacher's guide, are in italics.)

B Choose one of the three people and write a letter telling why you admire him or her.

I Simon Rodia wanted to be remembered for doing something good. What do you want people to remember about you?

I *Do you know anyone like Larry Walters? Some people have dreams of inventing things or conquering a task "because it's there." Describe someone who tries new things for the adventure or for the sense of accomplishment.*

E "The sky's the limit." If you had no limitations (education, money, or family obligations), what would your dream be? If you could do anything you wanted to do, what would it be?

E *Compare the lives of two famous people— performers, sports figures, or heroes. Describe the influences (people, events, motivations) that helped them to excel in their fields.*

LETTERS AND VERSES ABOUT WAR

(PAGES 111-120)

· ·

THEME SUMMARY

The first two letters are written by those who served their country. These letters are "last letters" to family members: Sullivan Ballou's letter conveys his feelings about family; his purpose is to write a last letter just in case he dies in battle. Sharon Lane writes of the daily details—of injuries and deaths, movies, schedules, her physical surroundings. Her letter is not written as a final correspondence; she did not expect to die. The last selection contains poetry written by a husband to his wife who is serving in the Persian Gulf War. All three selections reveal an appreciation for loved ones. (Note: "APO 96225" and "North Light," in *Expressions*, would make good companion pieces to these selections.)

· ·

STEP-BY-STEP LESSON PLAN

1. Ask the pre-reading questions:

   • Have you ever been away from loved ones? Did you miss family and friends? How did you cope?

   Start a discussion by giving examples of a time when you were away from home or relate a story about when a relative was away.

2. Read the purpose statement aloud to help students set a goal for reading:

   • As you read, think about who and what you would miss most if you were separated from loved ones.

3. Give students time to read each piece silently. Or you might want to read the first one aloud, review the purpose statement, and then assign the other readings.

4. Ask students to summarize the main idea of each reading. Then ask the following literal **L**, interpretive **I**, and critical **C** reading questions. (Questions that appear in the student anthology are in regular typeface. Additional questions, which appear only in this teacher's guide, are in italics.)

L Does each writer say how it feels to be in a war or to have a loved one in a war?

Answer: Sullivan Ballou says he is willing to lay down his life to help maintain the government. Sharon Lane does not discuss war or her part in it. George Albertini, Jr., says that his wife is very patriotic and believes in what she is doing. He prays for her safe return and writes her love verses to ease the pain of their separation.

L Which of the three writers has seen the most effects of war?

Answer: Sharon Lane, a nurse, deals daily with life and death. Her letter conveys the chaos and horror of caring for South Vietnamese and American soldiers wounded in the war.

C George Albertini, Jr., writes to his wife, "Your purpose gives hope to all free people, your cause is a noble one." Do you agree or disagree with this view of the Persian Gulf War? Explain.

Answer: Answers will vary; use as class discussion.

I Do you agree that you can say things in a letter that you cannot say in person? Why?

Answer: Yes; it is less threatening to be honest on paper than to talk face-to-face and get an immediate reaction to your words.

I *In Sharon Lane's letter, why do you think the Registrar's office made a game of guessing and took bets on the arrival of the 10,000th patient?*

Answer: This detail reveals how common injury and death are to the medical staff members in Vietnam. Their betting may seem cold and heartless, but it is a way to keep their sanity in the worst possible circumstances.

L *What promise does Sullivan Ballou make to his wife?*

Answer: He promises her that they will be together after death and that his spirit will always be near her in the gladdest days and in the darkest nights as a breeze upon her cheek, if the dead come back to earth.

5. End the lesson with activities that meet students' needs, interests, and learning goals.

· ·

ACTIVITIES

RHETORIC

Characterization

1. List the names of the three writers on the board. Ask students to identify similarities and differences such as:

   - the writer's "audience" (who received the letter)

   - the writer's purpose

   - the writer's attitude toward loved ones

2. Discuss how those receiving the letters might have reacted—Mrs. Ballou, Sharon Lane's parents, and Michelle Perna.

Language and Style

1. Read Sullivan Ballou's letter aloud. Stress his emotions and ask the students, "Do his words have more power when read aloud? Why?"

2. Characterize each writer's style. Why does Sharon Lane use fragments? Which pieces are emotional? Which are objective or factual? Which are poetic?

COMMUNICATION

Sharing Stories About War

1. If the students have war stories, use class time for sharing what they know or have heard about war.

2. Bring in a globe or world map to show locations such as Bull Run, Vietnam, and the Persian Gulf.

3. Follow up with a time line (brief historical overview) of these wars.

4. Bring in books such as *The Civil War: An Illustrated History*, *The Wall* (Vietnam Memorial), or other picture books of each war era.

Perception

1. Discuss with students the reversal of roles that has taken place in recent wars. Some examples include:

   - women actively participating in a war and not just taking care of wounded soldiers

   - women putting young children in day-care centers while they are away at war

   - husbands at home writing letters to their wives who are serving in a war

   - husbands taking care of their children while their wives serve in a war

2. Ask students to recall and share instances of role reversal among their families and friends during a recent war.

3. Ask students if they agree or disagree with this role reversal in times of war.

WRITING

The following assignments may be done in or out of class. **B** designates an assignment suitable for beginning writers; **I**, intermediate writers; **E**, more experienced writers. (Assignments that appear in the student anthology are in regular typeface. Additional assignments, which appear only in this teacher's guide, are in italics.)

B Have you ever been homesick? Write a journal entry for a date (day and year) when you missed your loved ones. Describe why you were away from home and how you felt.

I "Going off to war" is not as glamorous as it may sound. Besides facing danger, soldiers must deal with being away from what is familiar to them. Write a few paragraphs describing what you would miss most if you were to go to war.

I Write a letter using one of these points of view:

   - from Mrs. Sullivan Ballou after getting her husband's letter

   - to someone you need to say something to but cannot say in person

   - to someone you've left behind as you've gone off to war

E *Many people supported the troops who fought in the Persian Gulf War but did not believe the war itself was justified. Write two or three paragraphs explaining your views about this split in people's beliefs. Do you agree or disagree?*

Related videos include: Civil War—*Gone with the Wind, Glory*, or *The Civil War: An Illustrated History*; Vietnam—*The Deer Hunter, Apocalypse Now, Platoon*.

Contemporary's Whole Language Series

EXPRESSIONS

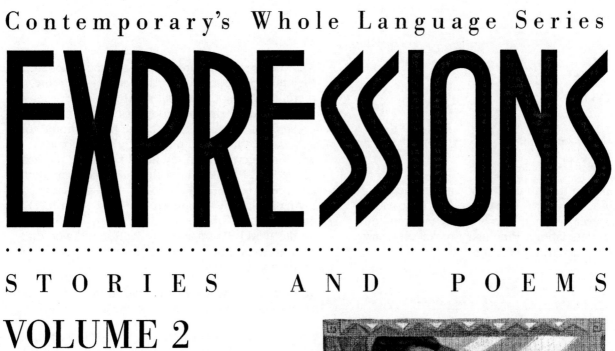

STORIES AND POEMS

VOLUME 2

.05

(PAGES 1-3)

. . . .

POEM SUMMARY

The speaker in this humorous poem feels that he'd be a fabulously wealthy bank president if he had a nickel for every woman who has ever rejected him but a penniless laborer if he had a nickel for every woman who has ever loved him.

. . . .

STEP-BY-STEP LESSON PLAN

1. Ask the pre-reading question:

   • Have you ever been unlucky in love?

Start a discussion by describing times in your own life when you were unlucky. Ask students how they felt in similar situations.

2. Read the purpose statement aloud to help students set a goal for reading:

   • As you read, imagine how the speaker feels. Does he mean everything he says?

3. Give students time to read the poem silently, or read the poem aloud to students.

4. Ask the following literal **L**, interpretive **I**, and critical **C** reading questions. (Questions that appear in the student anthology are in regular typeface. Additional questions, which appear only in this teacher's guide, are in italics.)

L When you read a poem, do not automatically pause at the end of each line. Instead, group words together in meaningful chunks. Pause as you would in normal conversation. The lines in ".05" could be rearranged to form three sentences. If you were putting the poem in sentence form, where would you punctuate with periods? Read the poem out loud, pausing longer at these points.

Answer: If students aren't used to reading poetry, they may pause too long at the end of each line, thereby missing the logical relationship between ideas. Guide their reading by writing the poem in prose form on a chalkboard. The poem should look as follows: "If I had a nickel for all the women who've rejected me in my life, I would be the head of the World Bank, with a flunkie to hold my derby as I prepared to fly chartered jet to sign a check giving India a new lease on life. If I had a nickel for all the women who've loved me in my life, I would be the World Bank's assistant janitor and wouldn't need to wear a derby. All I'd think about would be going home."

I How does the speaker feel about his relationships with women?

Answer: He feels negative about his relationships, suggesting that very few women have ever loved him.

I Is the speaker serious about what he says, or is he joking? How can you tell?

Answer: The manner in which the speaker laments his poor relationships with women suggests that he is exaggerating for comic effect but does, indeed, believe that he's been a failure with the opposite sex. (Other answers are possible.)

L What would the speaker do if he had a nickel for every woman who has ever rejected him? Contrast these actions with what he would do if he had a nickel for every woman who has ever loved him.

Answer: The speaker imagines peforming a great act of charity if he were wealthy and a self-centered act (thinking only about going home) if he were poor.

I What does the speaker mean when he says he would "sign a check / Giving India a new lease / On life"?

Answer: He means that he would have so much money that he could provide for all the starving, homeless people in India.

C *Why does the poet have the speaker use a lowercase rather than a capital "i" to refer to himself?*

Answer: The lowercase "i" supports the image of the speaker as a failure in matters of love. The speaker feels small, and thus a "small," or lowercase letter, is appropriate. (Other answers are possible.)

5. End the lesson with activities that meet students' needs, interests, and learning goals.

ACTIVITIES

LITERATURE

Hyperbole

1. Define *hyperbole* as an extravagant exaggeration used to make a point. Explain that writers expect readers to recognize that the exaggerations are not to be taken literally. Point out the two major hyperboles in the poem—that the speaker would be wealthy if he received a nickel every time a woman rejected him and destitute if he received a nickel every time a woman loved him.

2. Ask students for examples of hyperboles they have heard or used themselves, or suggest that they make up their own by describing common objects, situations, or events in an exaggerated fashion. Use the following examples as models:

   - The wrestler was a mountain of flesh.

   - The money that man spends on shoes could repay the national debt.

   - When my father lost his temper and began yelling, children for blocks around ran crying to their mothers and homeowners rushed to nail plywood over their windows.

3. Ask students why they think the speaker in ".05" used hyperbole to talk about his lack of success in love. Discuss how hyperbole can be used to create humor.

COMMUNICATION

Self-Perception

1. Explain that a person's self-image—how a person perceives himself or herself—affects other people's image of the person. Offer the following example:

   - A student who answers questions with an air of confidence will often receive a better evaluation than a student who gives the same answers but sounds doubtful.

Ask students to give examples of times when their image of another person was affected by the person's self-image.

2. The speaker in the poem feels that he has little chance of developing a good relationship with a woman. Ask students what he might be doing to communicate that he is unlovable. Ask what he might do to improve his self-image and others' image of him.

WRITING

The following assignments may be done in or out of class. **B** designates an assignment suitable for beginning writers; **I**, intermediate writers; **E**, more experienced writers. (Assignments that appear in the student anthology are in regular typeface. Additional assignments, which appear only in this teacher's guide, are in italics.)

B If the speaker were wealthy, he'd hire an assistant, fly in a private jet, and give a fortune to charity. Explain what you would do if you had millions of dollars.

I In your opinion, why have women rejected the speaker so often? Imagine that you are one of the women who rejected him. Write him a letter telling why you don't want to see him again. If you want, use the following beginning to get started:

"Dear John,
I'm sorry to say that I'm leaving you because you are just too . . ."

I *The speaker in the poem feels that he has been rejected by an unusually large number of women. Perhaps he has been attracted to the wrong kind of woman. Write a description of the kind of man or woman you're attracted to. Explain why you think this kind of person is right for you.*

E Write a poem in the same two-part form as ".05." Begin each part with "If I had a nickel / for every time . . ."

MY FATHER SITS IN THE DARK

(PAGES 5-11)

· ·

STORY SUMMARY

A son tells about his father's peculiar habit of sitting motionless in a darkened kitchen long after the rest of the family has gone to bed. Puzzled and worried by his father's strange behavior, the son makes several unsuccessful attempts to get his father to explain himself. Finally, late one night, the father makes a remark that gives the son a glimpse into his motives for sitting in the dark.

· ·

STEP-BY-STEP LESSON PLAN

1. Ask the pre-reading question:

   • How well do you really know the people closest to you?

To help students answer the question, lead the following activity: Have students write down the names of three friends or family members that they feel they know very well. Then ask them to write answers to the following questions:

   • What event would each person on your list consider to be the most important in his or her life?

   • What is each person's greatest hope or desire?

When students are finished, ask how many are sure that they answered each question the same as the listed friends or family members would. While some students probably will feel that they know the people on their lists well enough to answer the questions accurately, it's likely that other students will feel unsure of what the people on their list would say. Ask those who are unsure to discuss why they feel as they do. Follow up by suggesting that everyone ask the people on their lists if the answers are accurate.

2. Read the purpose statement aloud to help students set a goal for reading:

   • As you read, ask yourself why the father sits in the dark.

3. Give students time to read the story silently, or have students perform the story as readers' theater. Ask one student to read the narrative parts of the story and two other students to read the father-son dialogue in character.

4. Ask the following literal **L**, interpretive **I**, and critical **C** reading questions. (Questions that appear in the student anthology are in regular typeface. Additional questions, which appear only in this teacher's guide, are in italics.)

L What questions does the son keep asking his father? Why does he ask them?

Answer: The son asks, "Why don't you go to bed? What are you thinking about? What's wrong?" He asks these questions because he can't understand why his father sits in the dark, and he fears that his father is upset or worried about something.

L Where did the father live as a boy? Where does he live now?

Answer: As a boy, the father lived in Austria. Now he lives in the United States in an apartment with his family.

I How does the father feel about the past? How can you tell?

Answer: Some students may argue that the father is contented with his memories of the past. To support this interpretation, students may point to his insisting that nothing is bothering him and the son's description of his father as "too peaceful . . . just too peaceful, to be brooding." Students who notice that the father's brothers and parents are dead may argue that the father feels nostalgic or sad about the past.

I How do you think the writer of the story would answer the following question: How well does a person know the people he or she is close to? Explain your answer.

Answer: The story is primarily about a son's struggle to know and understand his father. The ending of the story, in which the father quietly refuses to specify what he is thinking about, suggests that the son's struggle will continue. Given the theme and the conclusion, it's logical to infer that the writer of the story would say that people don't know one another as well as they might think they do. (Other answers are possible.)

C *The writer of the story chooses his words very carefully. For example, he says that the father "looks too peaceful, too, well not contented, just too peaceful, to be brooding." Look up the meanings of* peaceful *and* contented. *What would a person who is feeling peaceful look like? What would a contented person look like? Why does the writer make a distinction between the two?*

Answer: A contented person appears satisfied, as though all his or her needs are fulfilled. A peaceful person appears to be at rest, undisturbed and untroubled. By having the son make a distinction between the two feelings, the author shows that the boy has puzzled long and hard about his father. (Other answers are possible.)

5. End the lesson with activities that meet students' needs, interests, and learning goals.

· ·

ACTIVITIES

LITERATURE

Character Motivation

1. Point out that it is important for readers to think about character motivation—the reasons that characters do what they do and say what they say. Ask students to think of questions that they would like to ask the son and the father. Use the following questions as examples:

   * *son*: Why is it so important to you to know what your father is thinking?

   * *father*: Why don't you either answer your son's questions or tell him to stop bothering you?

List students' answers on a chalkboard.

2. Ask two students to play the roles of the father and the son and a third student to play the role of an interviewer. The interviewer should ask the questions on the board; the other role-players should answer the questions in character.

COMMUNICATION

Withholding Feelings

1. Point out that neither character tells the other how he feels or why he behaves as he does. Though the son tells readers that he feels fear, annoyance, anger, and happiness, he never tells his father that he feels these emotions. The father never expresses any emotion at all toward his son. To make these points, read aloud the dialogue in the story, skipping over the son's narrative.

2. Tell students to think of a time when they refused to discuss their feelings with a family member who upset them. Then ask:

   * Why didn't you discuss your feelings?

   * What happened as a result of hiding your feelings?

   * If you had it to do over again, would you still hide your feelings? Why or why not?

3. Ask pairs of students to play the roles of the father and son. During the role-play, the father and son should explain what they're feeling. Discuss how different pairs interpret what the father and son might be feeling.

Interviewing

1. Ask students to interview someone who is a newcomer to the United States. (If your class consists of immigrants, have students interview each other.) Together, prepare a list of questions students might ask. Use the following questions as examples:

   * Where are you from?

   * What is your favorite place there? Describe it.

   * What are some of the most popular foods or dishes in your country?

2. Have students do oral or written presentations based on respondents' answers.

WRITING

The following assignments may be done in or out of class. **B** designates an assignment suitable for beginning writers; **I**, intermediate writers; **E**, more experienced writers. (Assignments that appear in the student anthology are in regular typeface. Additional assignments, which appear only in this teacher's guide, are in italics.)

B Imagine that you are the son in the story, and write a note to the father explaining why you are worried about him.

B *Imagine that you are the father, and write a note to your son telling what you are thinking about as you sit in the dark.*

I Have you ever been puzzled by something that someone close to you did? Describe the experience and your reaction to it.

I *The father seems to have pleasant memories of childhood in his native country. Describe your favorite childhood place in your native country.*

E Do you think that the son has a right to know what his father is thinking? Or does the father have a right to keep his thoughts to himself? Explain which view you agree with.

WHEN I HEAR YOUR NAME

(PAGES 12-13)

....

POEM SUMMARY

A speaker expresses powerful emotions for a loved one in a series of hyperboles involving the loved one's name. Addressing the special person, the speaker vows to spend eternity repeating the loved one's name.

....

STEP-BY-STEP LESSON PLAN

1. Ask the pre-reading question:

   • Have you ever had such strong feelings for someone that he or she was all you could think about?

To start the discussion, talk about a time when you had strong feelings—positive or negative— for someone. Encourage students to share their experiences.

2. Read the purpose statement aloud to help students set a goal for reading:

   • As you read, notice how the speaker uses exaggeration to make a point.

3. Give students time to read the poem silently, or ask a student to read the poem aloud with feeling, as if he or she were speaking the poem to a loved one.

4. Ask the following literal **L**, interpretive **I**, and critical **C** reading questions. (Questions that appear in the student anthology are in regular typeface. Additional questions, which appear only in this teacher's guide, are in italics.)

L Which statements in the poem are exaggerations?

Answer: Students should see that virtually every statement in the poem is a hyperbole, or extravagant exaggeration. (For a more detailed description of hyperbole, see page 75 of this *Teacher's Guide.*)

I What does the speaker mean by the statement "When I hear your name / I feel a little robbed of it"?

Answer: Hearing the loved one's name on another's lips is like being forced to share the loved one with the person who is speaking. (Other answers are possible.)

C *We are told how the speaker feels when hearing the name of the special person, but we are never told what the name is. Why might the poet have chosen not to give it?*

Answer: A name can have very different connotations for different people. Specifying a name might make the poem less effective, because any name the poet would give would have negative connotations for some readers. Also, the omission of the name makes the poem more universal. Readers can "fill in the blank" and imagine any names they choose—including the names of their own loved ones. (Other answers are possible.)

I *At the end of the poem, the speaker imagines being sentenced by God to repeat the special person's name "endlessly and forever." Does the speaker fear or welcome the sentence? How can you tell?*

Answer: Given the speaker's overwhelming love, it's likely he or she would welcome the sentence.

I *Is "When I Hear Your Name" a love poem? Why or why not? If it isn't a love poem, what other emotion might the speaker be feeling?*

Answer: Most students will consider "When I Hear Your Name" a love poem because the speaker professes feeling proud and happy when repeating the loved one's name. However, some students may argue that what the speaker feels is obsession rather than love.

5. End the lesson with activities that meet students' needs, interests, and learning goals.

....

ACTIVITIES

LITERATURE

Stanzas

1. Point out that the poem is divided into four units, or stanzas. If students are familiar with paragraphing, you might draw an analogy between paragraphs in prose and stanzas in poetry.

2. Have students summarize the main idea of each stanza so that they can see the logic underlying the stanza breaks.

3. Follow up by asking students to analyze the stanza breaks in another simply structured poem, such as ".05" (on page 1 of the student anthology).

IMAGERY

1. Explain that *imagery* refers to descriptive details that appeal to one or more of the five senses. The imagery in "When I Hear Your Name" appeals primarily to the sense of sound. Ask students to list details that, in their opinion, are particularly effective. Students may mention the following sound imagery:

Stanza 1

- hearing the name and what the half dozen letters mean

Stanza 2

- blasting down walls with the name

- shouting the name down wells and uttering it on mountains

- listening to the name echoed back

Stanza 3

- teaching birds to sing the name

- teaching men the madness of repeating the name

Stanza 4

- saying hello and begging bread with the name

Stanza 5

- answering questions in the other world with the name

- repeating the name endlessly and forever

COMMUNICATION

Gender and Communication

1. Ask students if they think the speaker of the poem is a man or a woman. Have them give reasons for their choice. (Though a woman wrote "When I Hear Your Name," the gender of the speaker of the poem is not identified. Either a man or a woman might speak the lines.)

2. Discuss verbal and nonverbal ways that men and women communicate that they are attracted to each other. To guide the discussion, ask the following questions:

- Are there differences between the ways in which men and women communicate their love for each other? If so, what are they?

- In your opinion, what is the cause of these differences? Are they inborn, or are they learned?

WRITING

The following assignments may be done in or out of class. **B** designates an assignment suitable for beginning writers; **I**, intermediate writers; **E**, more experienced writers. (Assignments that appear in the student anthology are in regular typeface. Additional assignments, which appear only in this teacher's guide, are in italics.)

B Is there someone you really like or dislike? Write a poem that explains how you feel. Begin by finishing this statement: "When I hear your name, I . . ."

I Imagine the speaker giving the poem to the person she has the compulsion for. How do you think the person would feel after reading it? Happy? Miserable? Frightened? Some other emotion? Explain.

E Describe a positive compulsion that you had for a person, place, or thing. How long did the compulsion last? How did you feel when it was over?

E *Add another verse to the middle of the poem. Begin by finishing the following statement: "My compulsion is . . ."*

MY TOCAYA

(PAGES 15-21)

· ·

STORY SUMMARY

A Mexican-American high school student describes the mysterious disappearance, apparent death, and then sudden reappearance of her *tocaya*, or namesake, a classmate of hers. Although she didn't know her *tocaya* well, the student has strong feelings about her and all the attention that she has attracted.

· ·

STEP-BY-STEP LESSON PLAN

1. Ask the pre-reading question:

   • Have you ever felt a mysterious connection to another person, even though you did not know the person very well?

To start a discussion, describe a time when you met someone for the first time and immediately sensed that you wanted to know more about the person. Discuss how occasionally people who seem to have nothing in common become close friends. Point out that sometimes people are drawn together because one has a trait or characteristic that the other lacks or desires.

2. Read the purpose question aloud to help students set a goal for reading:

   • As you read the story, ask yourself how you would describe the speaker's attitude toward the "other Patricia."

3. Give students time to read the story silently, or have students take turns reading the story aloud. Encourage students to read the narrator's lines in the breezy, informal style that characterizes her speech. Tell students that they should examine the feelings underlying what the girl says about herself and her *tocaya*. Ask if what she says completely explains her behavior and her attitude.

4. Ask the following literal **L**, interpretive **I**, and critical **C** reading questions. (Questions that appear in the student anthology are in regular typeface. Additional questions, which appear only in this teacher's guide, are in italics.)

L Where does the story take place? What details describe the neighborhood?

Answer: The story takes place in San Antonio, Texas. (Note the names of the newspapers that carry the story of the *tocaya*'s death.) The neighborhood seems to be Mexican-American. The characters speak Spanish and have Spanish names, some of the street names are Spanish, and the *tocaya*'s family owns a taco stand.

I Though the speaker doesn't say much about herself directly, her actions and attitude toward her *tocaya* tell a lot about her. What is the speaker like?

Answer: Like many teenagers, the speaker is very judgmental—she makes catty, critical remarks about her *tocaya* throughout the story. She also seems to be jealous of all the attention that Patricia Benavídez has gotten.

I *Where in the story does the speaker express sympathy for Patricia Benavídez? Why does she speak so harshly of Patricia if she actually feels sympathetic?*

Answer: The speaker feels sympathy when she speculates why her *tocaya* ran away: "Got tired of coming home [from her father's taco stand] stinking of crispy tacos. Well, no wonder she left. I wouldn't want to stink of crispy tacos neither. Who knows what she had to put up with. Maybe her father beat her. He beats her brother, I know that." The speaker sees herself as a tough, worldly person (though she isn't) and is therefore quick to disown sympathetic feelings. (Other answers are possible.)

I Why does the speaker call Patricia a "freak"?

Answer: The speaker thinks of her as a freak because Patricia wears high-heeled "glitter" shoes and rhinestone earrings, wants to be called Trish rather than a Spanish-sounding nickname, affects a British accent, and is younger than most of their classmates. In typical teenage fashion, the speaker disdains other teenagers who dress or speak differently from the clique she belongs to.

C The writer of the story has the speaker use "incorrect" grammar and swearwords. Why? How would it change the story if the speaker spoke "properly"? In your opinion, would it make the story better?

Answer: The swearwords and incorrect grammar are important in developing the sarcastic teenager's character. If she spoke "properly" and didn't swear, she wouldn't seem as real, and the story would be less believable. (Other answers are possible.)

I The speaker never has a chance to speak to Max, the teenager she has a crush on. Do you think Patricia told the truth about Max's interest in the speaker? Why or why not?

Answer: Some students will argue that the *tocaya*'s statements about Max Luna Luna's interest in the speaker should be taken at face value. Others may believe that Patricia, feeling like an outsider among her older classmates, fabricated Max's interest as a way of ingratiating herself with the speaker.

5. End the lesson with activities that meet students' needs, interests, and learning goals.

· ·

ACTIVITIES

LITERATURE

Character Development

1. Ask students how they form an impression of someone the first time they meet. What characteristics do they notice? Age? Clothing? Manner of speaking? Body language? List students' responses on a chalkboard.

2. Point out that the characteristics that students just named are also helpful in understanding fiction. A writer *develops*, or creates, believable characters using certain techniques. Readers can understand fictional people by answering the following questions:

   • What do the characters look like?

   • How do the characters speak?

   • What do the characters say about themselves?

   • What do the characters say to and about one another?

   • What does the narrator say about the characters?

   • What do the characters do?

   • Based on the answers to these questions, what can I conclude about the characters?

List the above questions on a chalkboard.

3. Have students analyze the narrator's personality by answering each of the questions on the list.

COMMUNICATION

Varying Perceptions

1. Point out that people may interpret the same facts or behavior very differently. For example, the *tocaya* in the story probably believes that wearing high heels makes her look older and sophisticated, while the narrator believes that the high heels make the girl look cheap.

2. Using the example above as a model, have students give the narrator's and the *tocaya*'s perceptions of the following actions:

   • Patricia Benavídez's calling herself Trish and affecting a British accent

   • Patricia's running away from home and reappearing

   • the narrator's becoming friends with Patricia because of Max Luna Luna

3. Follow up by asking students to describe a time when their perceptions of an event or person were different from someone else's. Ask what caused the difference and whether problems resulted from varying perceptions.

WRITING

The following assignments may be done in or out of class. **B** designates an assignment suitable for beginning writers; **I**, intermediate writers; **E**, more experienced writers. (Assignments that appear in the student anthology are in regular typeface. Additional assignments, which appear only in this teacher's guide, are in italics.)

B Why did Patricia Benavídez leave home? Imagine that you are she, and write a letter explaining why you are leaving.

I Where do you think Patricia Benavídez was while everyone was looking for her? Use your imagination to describe the time she spent away from home. Explain why she came back.

I *Everything that we know about Patricia Benavídez comes from the narrator, who admits she doesn't know the girl well. Describe what you think Patricia's life was like in school, at work, and at home.*

E Patricia Benavídez's "return from the dead" would be front-page news. Write a short news story giving the facts about her return. Give your story an attention-grabbing headline.

SMALL SONG FOR DADDY

(PAGES 22-23)

· ·

POEM SUMMARY

The speaker of the poem is awakened by his infant daughter at 1:00 A.M. As he holds her, he marvels at the sound of her small voice and at the sense of wonder she feels for the everyday objects around her. He reflects that she is completely unaware that her wordless song fills a need within him.

· ·

STEP-BY-STEP LESSON PLAN

1. Ask the pre-reading question:

   • Do fathers feel different toward their daughters than toward their sons?

To start a discussion, describe how you treat your own children or how you were treated as a child. Invite students to share their experiences as parents or children.

2. Read the purpose statement aloud to help students set a goal for reading:

   • As you read, think about the father's emotions.

3. Give students time to read the poem silently, or ask a student to read the poem aloud.

4. Ask the following literal **L**, interpretive **I**, and critical **C** reading questions. (Questions that appear in the student anthology are in regular typeface. Additional questions, which appear only in this teacher's guide, are in italics.)

I The poem is about a daughter. How old do you think she is? What details give you clues about her age?

Answer: She is an infant. She has some control over her arms and legs and looks closely at objects, but she doesn't know how to talk yet.

L Is the daughter upset, or is she contented? What details tell you so?

Answer: She is contented. She plays with the hair on her father's chest, wiggles her toes, and sings softly.

I What do you think the daughter's song sounds like?

Answer: Her song probably consists of soft cooing or murmuring.

I *Have you ever lived in a house with young children? If so, how did you feel when they awakened you during the night? How did they behave? Compare your experience with that of the father and daughter in the poem.*

Answer: Answers will vary, but students are likely to agree that most adults are a little irritated and most young children are upset or unhappy when awakened during the night. In contrast, the father and daughter in the poem are sharing a positive and tender moment.

I At the end of the poem, why does the father call the baby's song "her particular song"? Why do you think he might be so much in need of his daughter's song?

Answer: The father feels that his daughter's sounds are different from those of any other baby. Knowing that his daughter loves and depends on him probably helps the father feel motivated to cope with whatever problems he faces at work or in other aspects of his life. (Other answers are possible.)

I What do you imagine happened after the events in the poem? Did the daughter go quickly back to sleep? How did the father feel after her song ended?

Answer: Students' opinions may vary about whether the baby went quickly back to sleep. On the one hand, she seems calm and contented and perhaps ready to sleep. On the other, she woke up for some reason, and whatever it is may keep her awake. Since the father says he is in need of her song, we can assume that it makes him feel better while she is singing it. He may or may not feel sad or upset again after the song ends.

C *Read the poem aloud, listening for words that begin or end with the letters s or sh. Why are these fitting sounds to use in a poem about a father and baby communicating during the night?*

Answer: The sounds are as soft and hushed as a baby's song or as the gentle tone a father might adopt when talking with his infant during the night.

5. End the lesson with activities that meet students' needs, interests, and learning goals.

ACTIVITIES

LITERATURE

Similes

1. Point out that a writer may compare the unfamiliar to the familiar to help readers understand or picture an idea. For example, in "Small Song for Daddy" W. D. Ehrhart compares the sound of his daughter's voice (something unfamiliar to readers) to the sound of "water striking stone" (something he knows many readers will have heard). Have students reread Ehrhart's comparison, which appears in lines 9–10.

2. Explain that Ehrhart's description is a *simile*, a comparison that includes *like*, *than*, or *as*. Provide students with practice in identifying similes by having them analyze what is compared in each of the following sentences:

   • The sudden volley of hail stung like a thousand bees.

   • His glare was colder than a January night in Juneau.

   • The visitors were as welcome as the first robin in spring.

3. Ask students to make up similes to describe the following situations. Encourage students to come up with several ideas for each.

   • As he sat in the dentist's waiting room, his heart pounded like _____.

   • The politician's speech seemed to last longer than _____.

   • The July afternoon was as hot as _____.

COMMUNICATION

Communication Between Parents and Children

1. Although the daughter in the poem cannot speak, she does communicate her feelings nonverbally, through her behavior. Begin a discussion by asking students how they think the baby feels. What nonverbal cues, or body language, reveal her feelings? What nonverbal cues might the father use to communicate his love for his daughter?

2. Although the father and daughter communicate well, they may experience difficulty communicating when the daughter grows older and more independent. Ask the following questions to generate discussion about communication barriers between parents and their children and ways to overcome them.

   • What barriers, or obstacles, sometimes interfere with communication between parents and their teenage children?

   • What advice would you give the father in the poem to help him continue to communicate effectively with his daughter as she grows older?

   • What advice would you give the daughter?

WRITING

The following assignments may be done in or out of class. **B** indicates an assignment suitable for beginning writers; **I**, intermediate writers; **E**, more experienced writers. (Assignments that appear in the student anthology are in regular typeface. Additional assignments, which appear only in this teacher's guide, are in italics.)

B The father in the poem focuses on describing his daughter's voice. Describe someone you admire or love. In your description, focus on one characteristic also, such as voice, eyes, or gestures.

I The father says he is "much in need" of his daughter's song. What happened during the day to make him need her song that night? Use your imagination, and describe the father's day.

E What do you think the father is feeling most strongly in this poem? Describe a situation in which you felt the same emotion.

E *Imagine that you are writing to new parents who are about to take their infant home from the hospital. Explain step-by-step what the parents should do when their newborn awakens and cries during the night.*

CROSSING SPIDER CREEK

(PAGES 25-28)

· ·

STORY SUMMARY

A seriously injured man tries to urge his frightened horse across a flooded mountain stream. After two failed attempts, he realizes he has the strength to make only one more try. As he prepares to cross, he thinks of his wife, Carol, and wonders if he will ever see her again.

· ·

STEP-BY-STEP LESSON PLAN

1. Ask the pre-reading questions:

   • Have you ever been in a dangerous situation—perhaps even a life-threatening one? What thoughts raced through your mind? Did you concentrate on what was happening, or did you find yourself thinking about loved ones and friends?

Start a discussion by talking about the thoughts that raced through your mind during a time when you were in danger. Ask students to recall and describe their thoughts in times of great danger.

2. Read the purpose statement aloud to help students set a goal for reading:

   • As you read the story, notice what the man thinks about as he faces a life-or-death situation.

3. Give students time to read the story silently, or ask a student to read the story aloud.

4. Ask the following literal **L**, interpretive **I**, and critical **C** reading questions. (Questions that appear in the student anthology are in regular typeface. Additional questions, which appear only in this teacher's guide, are in italics.)

L Why is it important for Tom to cross Spider Creek? What will happen to him if he is unable to?

Answer: Tom has a serious leg break that is causing him to bleed. If he cannot cross the creek to get help, he will probably bleed to death.

I Why is Tom having difficulty making his horse cross the creek?

Answer: The water level has risen, and the horse is frightened by the smell of blood.

L Why is Tom alone in the mountains?

Answer: He likes the solitude.

I Tom thinks about trying to shoot the horse if he falls off. He believes it would be best for Carol, his wife, if he and the horse were found dead together. Why does he think so?

Answer: Since the horse belongs to Carol, she might hold it—and herself—responsible for Tom's death. (Other answers are possible.)

I In your opinion, how does Tom's ordeal end? Does he make it across the creek, or doesn't he? Give reasons for your answer.

Answer: Some students may argue that Tom will make it across the creek because he is calm, knowledgeable, courageous, and determined. Other students may argue that Tom will fail because the young horse is too nervous to cross.

C *Why do you think the writer ended the story without telling whether Tom crossed the creek?*

Answer: The writer may have been more interested in the psychology of the situation—what Tom thinks and feels—than in plot development—what happens. (Other answers are possible.)

C *In your opinion, would the story be better if you were told whether Tom made it across the creek? Why or why not?*

Answer: Some students may be frustrated by the open ending and feel that the writer should have told what happened to Tom. Other students may feel that the open ending makes the story more effective by allowing readers to draw their own conclusions.

5. End the lesson with activities that meet students' needs, interests, and learning goals.

····························

ACTIVITIES

LITERATURE

Conflict

1. Explain that there are two major kinds of conflict in literature: *External conflicts* are physical or verbal struggles between two or more characters or a physical struggle between a character and a force of nature. *Internal conflicts* are psychological struggles. These inner struggles may involve the conscience or conflicting emotions. External conflicts often cause internal conflicts.

2. Give the following examples of each type of conflict. Ask students to add their own examples.

External Conflicts

- soldiers fighting

- a parent and a child arguing over the child's bedtime

- emergency room doctors and nurses trying to save an accident victim's life

- homeowners boarding up windows just before a hurricane hits their area

Internal Conflicts

- a spouse struggling to decide whether to file for divorce

- a person trying to accept that he or she may not recover from an illness

- a soldier trying to come to grips with a death he or she has caused

3. Ask students to describe the external and internal conflicts in the story.

COMMUNICATION

Problem Solving

1. Point out to students that Tom has shown courage in his fight to stay alive. Despite a broken and badly bleeding leg, he has managed to get on his horse to try to summon help. As the story ends, he is faced with a deep, cold creek and a horse that is afraid to cross. The campground and safety are only twenty minutes away on the other side of the creek.

2. Divide the class into groups. Have each group define Tom's problem. Is it crossing the creek? Staying alive? Summoning help? Point out that each definition of the problem suggests different kinds of solutions.

3. Once each group has decided on a definition, ask group members to brainstorm solutions to Tom's problem. Have groups report their solutions to the class as a whole.

WRITING

The following assignments may be done in or out of class. **B** designates an assignment suitable for beginning writers; **I**, intermediate writers; **E**, more experienced writers. (Assignments that appear in the student anthology are in regular typeface. Additional assignments, which appear only in this teacher's guide, are in italics.)

B Imagine that you are Tom, and write a note to Carol to be found if you don't make it across the creek. Tell her what you were thinking after you failed to cross the creek for the second time.

I How do you think Carol feels when Tom prepares for a trip into the mountains? Write a dialogue between Carol and Tom in which she expresses her emotions.

I *Suppose that Tom did not survive his attempt to reach help. Imagine that you are a reporter for the newspaper that covers the Spider Creek area, and write a news story about Tom and his accident.*

E Write a new conclusion for the story. Tell what happened when Tom attempted to cross the creek for the third and last time. Try to make your writing sound like the story writer's.

E *Write an additional paragraph or two for the story, telling how Tom was injured. Look for clues in the story. Try to make your writing sound like the writer's.*

MOTHER

(PAGES 29-31)

. . . .

POEM SUMMARY

A daughter returns to her mother's home after the parent dies. As the daughter walks through the house, she wishes she could see her mother one more time. The daughter seems to hear the mother's voice as she sits next to her empty chair. (Note: "Leaves," pages 45–47 of the student anthology, is about a similar situation—an adult child reminiscing about a parent. It would make a good companion piece to this poem.)

. . . .

STEP-BY-STEP LESSON PLAN

1. Ask the pre-reading question:

   • Has someone's death ever given you the feeling that things were left unsaid or not done?

To start a discussion, describe the loss of someone close to you and how you felt about being unable to talk with the person. Ask students to describe similar events in their own lives.

2. Read the purpose statement aloud to help students set a goal for reading:

   • As you read, think about the speaker's feelings toward her mother and her death.

3. Give students time to read the poem silently, or ask a student to read the poem aloud.

4. Ask the following literal **L**, interpretive **I**, and critical **C** reading questions. (Questions that appear in the student anthology are in regular typeface. Additional questions, which appear only in this teacher's guide, are in italics.)

L What does the daughter think about as she walks through her mother's house?

Answer: The daughter thinks about what she and her mother would do if they could be together one more time and all the things that she misses about her mother.

I What does the daughter miss most about her mother?

Answer: The daughter mentions several things that she misses: her mother's "silly welcome-rhyme," "happy tears," "eager questioning," and "cheery song." What the daughter misses the most is talking about her problems with her mother. Note that the poem opens with the line "I wish that I could talk with her again" and ends with the daughter's imagining her mother speaking with her.

I Why does the daughter sit next to her mother's empty chair?

Answer: This appears to be the place she always sat when she and her mother had a serious conversation.

I The daughter says nothing about her father. In your experience, are daughters usually closer to their mothers or to their fathers? Why?

Answer: Students' answers will vary. Encourage female students to discuss their roles as daughters and mothers. Encourage male students to discuss their roles as fathers of daughters and sons of mothers.

C *How does the tone, or feeling, of the poem change in the last line?*

Answer: For most of the poem, the tone is sad. The feeling expressed in the last line, however, is different. The speaker appears to feel encouraged by the advice she imagines her mother giving her, and the tone is upbeat and optimistic. (Other answers are possible.)

5. End the lesson with activities that meet students' needs, interests, and learning goals.

. . . .

ACTIVITIES

LITERATURE

Stanzas and Transitions

1. Point out that the poem is divided into three units, or stanzas. (For a more detailed discussion of stanzas, see pages 78–79 of this *Teacher's Guide.*) Ask:

   • What is the main idea of each stanza?

Students should see that each stanza develops a new thought in much the same way that a paragraph does in prose writing.

2. To help students see how the stanzas relate to each other, tell them to read the first line of the first and second stanzas. Note that the two stanzas parallel each other, the first one describing positive experiences, the second one describing experiences "that will never be." Point out that the first line of the second stanza acts as a *transition*, a word or group of words that connect ideas and show logical relationships. In this case, the transition prepares readers for the shift from wishful thinking to harsh reality.

3. Help students see the importance of the transition by reading the first two stanzas aloud without it. Students should notice that the omission makes the shift in ideas difficult to follow.

4. Discuss the actions that occur in the last stanza—the speaker's walking through the house and sitting next to her mother's chair—and how these actions prepare readers for the practical, down-to-earth statement made in the last line.

COMMUNICATION

Being a Good Listener

1. Ask students to look closely at the poem for clues about how the speaker and her mother talked together about important things. Help students see that the speaker focuses on her side of the conversations with her mother. The only thing she mentions about her mother's side is her "eager questions." Ask:

   - Which did the daughter value more—her mother's advice or ability to listen? Give reasons for your answer.

Students should see that the daughter placed more value on her mother's ability to listen. The following lines support this idea:

Stanza 1

   - "And she would let me talk until the parts / Fitted together."

Stanza 2

   - "So now I have come home to emptiness: / . . . No eager questioning. . . ."

2. Point out to students that good listening is an important part of good communication—and that asking the right questions is an important part of good listening. Explain that a good listener can help a speaker better understand his or her own thoughts. For example, the mother in the poem apparently helped her daughter work out problems by being sympathetic and asking the right questions.

3. Ask students to give examples of the kinds of questions that help people explore their own thoughts and feelings. Use the following questions to help students get started:

   - Can you tell me more about _____?

   - Why do you say that?

   - When you say _____, do you mean _____, or do you mean _____?

   - How do you feel when _____?

WRITING

The following assignments may be done in or out of class. **B** designates an assignment suitable for beginning writers; **I**, intermediate writers; **E**, more experienced writers. (Assignments that appear in the student anthology are in regular typeface. Additional assignments, which appear only in this teacher's guide, are in italics.)

B The daughter looked forward to her mother's "silly welcome-rhyme," "happy tears," and "eager questioning." List several small things that you look forward to whenever you enter some special or familiar place—your home, a friend's house, a favorite store or restaurant, a co-worker's office. Try to include sights, smells, and sounds.

I Write a conversation between the daughter and her mother. Imagine that they are discussing the daughter's life and one of the "parts that don't make sense." What problem might the daughter wish to discuss? What advice would the mother give?

I *The daughter says that she has been away from her mother for ten years. Describe where you imagine the daughter has been and why she was unable to visit her mother.*

E In the last two lines, the daughter imagines her mother talking to her. Does the daughter feel comforted by these imagined words, or do they upset her? Why do you think she feels this way?

E *Imagine that you are the daughter and that you have a daughter of your own. Write your daughter a letter while you are at your mother's house. Describe what you are feeling, and tell your daughter the kind of mother you want her to be.*

TRIP IN A SUMMER DRESS

(PAGES 33-44)

· ·

STORY SUMMARY

A young woman, about to be wed, is taking an overnight bus trip from Texas to her fiancé's home in Arkansas. On the bus ride, she reminisces about her past. She was an unwed mother at the age of fifteen, and her son has been raised to think that she is his sister. As the young woman rides, she wrestles with her desire to return and claim her son.

· ·

STEP-BY-STEP LESSON PLAN

1. Ask the pre-reading question:

   • Have you ever had trouble making an important decision?

To start a discussion, describe a time when you faced a dilemma and how you ultimately solved it. Explain that the main character of "Trip in a Summer Dress" is struggling to make a difficult decision.

2. Read the purpose statement aloud to help students set a goal for reading:

   • As you read, think about how [the young woman in the story] feels. In your opinion, does she make the right choice?

3. Give students time to read the story silently, or have students take turns reading the story aloud.

4. Ask the following literal **L**, interpretive **I**, and critical **C** reading questions. (Questions that appear in the student anthology are in regular typeface. Additional questions, which appear only in this teacher's guide, are in italics.)

L Where is the young woman in the story going? Why is she going there?

Answer: The young woman is traveling from Texas to her finacé's home in Arkansas to get married.

L The young woman says, "The day I said yes to [agreed to marry] Bill Richards I set my plan a-going." What was her plan? Why didn't she stick to it?

Answer: Her plan was to tell her son, Matthew, the truth about his parentage; claim him as her son; and marry Bill Richards. She doesn't stick to her plan because she's afraid of hurting her son and losing Bill.

I *The young woman says that Bill Richards thinks marriages are made in heaven. Do you think she agrees or disagrees? What does she say that supports your opinion?*

Answer: The young woman would probably disagree with Bill Richards's statement. She seems to be marrying him for practical rather than romantic reasons, and she worries about "how it's going to be in Eureka Springs with [the statue of] Christ looking right into the kitchen window when I'm kissing Bill . . . Him knowing all the time [the truth about Matthew's parentage]. . . ." (Other answers are possible.)

C Why does the young woman call Matthew's attention to the birds in the park? What do the mother and baby cowbird represent?

Answer: The mother cowbird, which leaves its young temporarily in the care of others, represents the young woman, who's leaving her son in her mother's care. The baby cowbird represents Matthew.

I What does the young woman plan to do when she goes into the telephone booth in Huntsville? What does she actually do? Why do you think she changed her mind?

Answer: The young woman plans to tell her mother that she wants to keep Matthew and tell Bill Richards the truth. Once she hears her mother's voice, however, she loses courage. In addition, the young woman might have begun to question the wisdom of her plan after spending time with the child on the bus. She may be wondering if Bill would grow to resent Matthew in the same way Rex resents the little girl. (Other answers are possible.)

I In your opinion, has the young woman chosen the right future for herself? For her son?

Answer: Students' answers will vary. Some students will feel strongly that both the young woman and her son are better off living out the lie to retain the son's stable, loving home and the young woman's fresh start. Other students will argue that the young couple's and Matthew's futures are jeopardized by the lie.

5. End the lesson with activities that meet students' needs, interests, and learning goals.

ACTIVITIES

LITERATURE

Symbolism

1. Define *symbol* as an object or action that signifies more than itself. Have students discuss the following common symbols and what they generally represent in the United States: a wedding ring, a cross on the front of a church, an American flag.

2. Explain that "Trip in a Summer Dress" contains several symbols. For example, the mother cowbird and baby cowbird represent the young woman and her relationship with her son.

3. Together, discuss the meaning of the following symbols, which appear in the story:

   - sleeveless dress (represents the young woman's vulnerability and lack of foresight)

   - aviary job "feeding fuzzy orphans" (represents the young woman's nurturing nature and foreshadows her relationship with Matthew)

   - dream about Moses' sister (represents the young woman's ambivalent feelings about leaving her son with her mother)

   - statue of Christ looking into the kitchen (represents the young woman's guilt)

   - sudden cold front (represents for the young woman the harshness of life without her child)

   - trip (represents a psychological as well as physical journey; pun on *trip* as *journey* and *err*)

COMMUNICATION

Decision Making

1. Point out that the plot of "Trip in a Summer Dress" hinges on the young woman's accidental pregnancy. Her future is set into motion when she fails to make a decision and becomes pregnant. As she herself puts it, "What happened was just a mistake I made because I'd never given much thought to that kind of thing and when the time came it caught me without my mind made up one way or the other."

2. Ask students to make a list of decisions the young woman makes before and during the course of the story. Discuss what alternatives she had at each decision point and what students would have decided in similar circumstances.

3. Help students analyze their own decision-making styles by asking the following questions:

   - Do you carefully weigh all the evidence and arguments before you make a decision?

   - Do you ask for advice from others?

   - Do you wait until the last minute to make decisions?

   - Do you often regret decisions you have made?

Together, identify good decision-making techniques that you've learned through experience.

WRITING

The following assignments may be done in or out of class. **B** designates an assignment suitable for beginning writers; **I**, intermediate writers; **E**, more experienced writers. (Assignments that appear in the student anthology are in regular typeface. Additional assignments, which appear only in this teacher's guide, are in italics.)

B In your opinion, who was right—the young woman or her mother? Make a list of reasons why you agree with the person. Organize the list so that it begins with the weakest, or least convincing, reason and ends with the strongest, or most convincing, reason.

I Like the young woman in the story, we all have to make difficult decisions from time to time. Write about a hard choice you once had to make. Explain how you felt and whether you were happy with your decision.

E Imagine that you are the young woman. Write a page in your diary explaining how you feel as the bus nears Bill Richards and your new home in Eureka Springs.

E *Imagine that you are Matthew, that you are now an adult, and that you have just learned that the woman you thought was your sister is actually your mother. Write a letter to your mother asking why she left you and explaining how you feel.*

LEAVES
(PAGES 45-47)

· ·

POEM SUMMARY

A son describes cooking with grape leaves that his father picked just before he died. The leaves trigger a memory of other mementos—notes and letters that his father wrote and left behind. In a final reminder, the son discovers from his mother that he inherited his love of poetry from his father. (Note: "Mother," pages 29–31 of the student anthology, is about a similar situation—an adult child reminiscing about a parent. It would make a good companion piece to this poem.)

· ·

STEP-BY-STEP LESSON PLAN

1. Ask the pre-reading question:

   • Have you ever treasured an object because it reminds you of a loved one who's now gone?

To start the discussion, describe a small memento that you keep to remember a relative or a friend. Ask students to describe similar objects of their own.

2. Read the purpose statement aloud to help students set a goal for reading:

   • As you read, think about the father's influence on his son.

3. Give students time to read the poem silently, or ask a student to read the poem aloud.

4. Ask the following literal **L**, interpretive **I**, and critical **C** reading questions. (Questions that appear in the student anthology are in regular typeface. Additional questions, which appear only in this teacher's guide, are in italics.)

L How long has the speaker's father been dead? What was the father's native language?

Answer: The father has been dead for over five years. His native language was Arabic.

I What things has the speaker saved as reminders of his father?

Answer: frozen grape leaves, notes, and letters

I The father had difficulty writing in English. What message did he write on the piece of tablet paper? What does the message tell you about him?

Answer: Transcribed into standard English, his message is "To my dear grandchildren, David and Laura, from their Jido." One can conclude from the message that he must have loved his grandchildren very much to have made the effort to write to them in English.

I What influence has the father had on the speaker?

Answer: The speaker says that he got his love of poetry from his father. In addition, the father probably influenced the son's choice of food (the traditional dish of stuffed grape leaves) and instilled in his son an interest in Arabic. (Other answers are possible.)

C *In the last lines of the poem, the speaker says, "Even now, at night, I sometimes / get out the Arabic grammar book / though it seems so late." What is the word "late" describing? The speaker's attempt to learn Arabic so late in life? Something else?*

Answer: Students' answers may vary; the ambiguity of the line admits a variety of interpretations. In addition to describing the speaker's attempt to learn Arabic late in life, the word *late* might also describe the speaker's desire to remember his father (and, by extension, his Arabic roots) and his father's poetry.

C *In your opinion, why does the poet include part of the letter from Charles Atlas to his father?*

Answer: The letter shows another side of his father—the naive young man who, in a desire to improve himself, answers the ads in the backs of magazines. (Other answers are possible.)

C *Why do you think the poet chose to title the poem "Leaves" rather than "Memories of My Father" or something else?*

Answer: Students' answers may vary. "Leaves" obviously refers to the grape leaves that trigger the memories of his father, but it may also refer to the father's note and letters or to fallen leaves and the passage of time.

5. End the lesson with activities that meet students' needs, interests, and learning goals.

. . . .

ACTIVITIES

LITERATURE

Narrative Structure

1. It's likely that the structure of the poem made it difficult for some students to follow. Point out the lack of transitions, and ask students if their absence posed problems.

2. Define *montage* as a collection of seemingly unrelated images and ideas that share a "hidden," or underlying, meaning. Have students identify the central image of the first stanza (grape leaves) and the second stanza (the father's note and letters). Ask the following questions:

   • What do the grape leaves, note, and letters have in common?

   • What triggered the son's memory of the note and letters?

Students should see that the grape leaves picked by the father remind the son of another type of leaf—the paper that his father wrote on.

3. Have students identify the central images of the third stanza—the poems and Arabic grammar book. Wrap up the discussion by asking the following questions:

   • What is the underlying connection between all the images in the poem?

   • In your opinion, would the poem be better if transitions were added between stanzas? Why or why not?

COMMUNICATION

Communication Barriers

1. Point out to students that the father in "Leaves" has a communication barrier to overcome. Because his native language is Arabic, he has difficulty writing in (and probably speaking) English.

2. Ask students if they have a grandparent or parent with whom they sometimes have difficulty communicating because English is not the older person's native language. Have students describe their communication problems and how they solve them. If English is not the first language of students themselves, ask them about problems they encounter communicating in English.

3. Point out that cultural differences may also serve as barriers to communication. For example, in some cultures maintaining steady eye contact during conversation is considered to be a sign of sincere interest, while in other cultures steady eye contact is considered to be impolite. This disparity can cause individuals from different cultures to misunderstand each other's intended message. Ask students to name other cultural barriers to communication and to discuss specific ways to overcome them.

WRITING

The following assignments may be done in or out of class. **B** designates an assignment suitable for beginning writers; **I**, intermediate writers; **E**, more experienced writers. (Questions that appear in the student anthology are in regular typeface. Additional questions, which appear only in this teacher's guide, are in italics.)

B The speaker got a love of poetry from his father. What likes (or dislikes) have your parents or other family members passed on to you? Describe a few.

I What objects do you keep in memory of a loved one? Describe one, telling who the object reminds you of and how it makes you feel.

I *Does preparing a particular dish remind you of someone? Describe how the dish is prepared, whom it reminds you of, and why it reminds you of the person. If an activity other than cooking triggers your memory of a loved one, write about that activity and the person you remember.*

E The speaker has saved a short written message for his children to remember their grandfather by. What message would you like to leave behind? Think of someone you are close to. Write the person a letter to be opened after your death.

E *Using your imagination and details from the poem, write a short biography of the speaker's father. Where did he come from? Where did he live? How did he earn a living? What was his family like?*

SCISSORS

(PAGES 49-61)

· ·

STORY SUMMARY

When Louise brings her three-year-old son, Robbie, into Harold's empty barbershop for a haircut, the two adults talk for the first time in years. Their conversation reveals that he and the married woman once had a love affair—and that Robbie is their son. As Louise and Robbie prepare to go, Saul Bernstein enters the shop. Noticing that Harold appears to be upset and distracted after the mother and son leave, Saul convinces Harold to close the shop and go for a beer and hamburger.

· ·

STEP-BY-STEP LESSON PLAN

1. Ask the pre-reading question:

   • How does it feel to talk to someone you used to love and haven't seen in a long time?

Start a discussion by asking students why running into an old acquaintance is sometimes awkward.

2. Read the purpose statement aloud to help students set a goal for reading:

   • As you read, look for clues that tell you about [Harold and Louise's] earlier relationship.

3. Give students time to read the story silently, or have students perform the story as readers' theater. Ask one student to read the narrative parts of the story and four other students to read the parts of Louise, Harold, Robbie, and Saul.

4. Ask the following literal **L**, interpretive **I**, and critical **C** reading questions. (Questions that appear in the student anthology are in regular typeface. Additional questions, which appear only in this teacher's guide, are in italics.)

L What is the first clue in the story that tells you Harold and Louise were once close?

Answer: Louise's kissing Harold on the cheek. (Other answers are possible.)

I *Describe Harold's behavior while Louise is in the shop. How would you describe Louise's behavior?*

Answer: Harold seems embarrassed, ill at ease, and confused, as though he's not sure how to react to Louise. She seems nervous and too talkative, as though she's talking to avoid an awkward silence or to keep Harold from saying something.

I How did Harold used to feel about Louise? Have his feelings changed?

Answer: Harold used to love Louise, and his behavior and thoughts indicate that he still has deep feelings for her. For example, he wants to stare at her when she first comes into the shop, has trouble steadying the tremble in his knees and hands as they talk, thinks that she is as beautiful (and crazy) as ever, and reminisces about a dinner when he was perfectly happy just being with her.

I How did Louise used to feel about Harold? How does she feel now? What does she think of her husband?

Answer: Louise used to love Harold but ultimately broke off their relationship because she felt he was too timid and conservative. Her feelings about Harold haven't changed—she still believes he is too mild. Louise seems to think that George, her husband, is out of touch with her—and life.

I Who is Robbie's father? What clues in the story tell you this?

Answer: The following clues indicate that Harold is Robbie's father: Louise's asking for Robbie's hair to be cut "sort of like a normal boy," hinting that something about Robbie is abnormal; Harold's nervousness while cutting Robbie's hair and his looking at their and Louise's reflections in the wall mirrors; Louise's pointing out that Robbie's hair and eyes look like Harold's; Harold's touching his lips to his fingers and then lightly touching the boy's cheek.

I *Why does Louise feel that the universe is a practical joke? Why does Harold disagree?*

Answer: Louise feels cheated; she expected certain things out of life that she didn't get. Harold, on the other hand, thinks that life is too complicated for anyone to have expectations.

I How much does Saul know about Harold and Louise's former relationship? How can you tell?

Answer: Saul seems to know or sense the significance of Harold and Louise's past relationship when he attempts to comfort Harold by getting him to leave the shop and when he says he knows that Harold used to know Louise.

C Why did the author include so much description of the hot-air balloon and the Tulip Days promotion?

Answer: The failure of the Tulip Days promotions parallels Harold's failed relationship with Louise, showing that Harold is ineffectual in both his professional and personal lives.

5. End the lesson with activities that meet students' needs, interests, and learning goals.

·······································

ACTIVITIES

LITERATURE

Foreshadowing

1. Point out that writers sometimes use *foreshadowing*—hints about what will happen in a plot—to involve readers in their stories. Readers stay with a story to see if they have correctly guessed what will happen.

2. To ensure that students understand foreshadowing, ask the following questions:

   • At what point in the story did you think Harold and Louise were once in love? At what point were you sure?

   • At what point did you think that Robbie was Harold's son? At what point were you sure?

   • At what point did you think that Saul knew about Harold and Louise's past relationship? At what point were you sure?

3. Discuss foreshadowing as a device to capture and hold readers' interest. Ask whether foreshadowing piqued students' curiosity in the characters and plot of "Scissors."

COMMUNICATION

Nonverbal Communication

1. Explain that there are different ways that people may communicate how they feel. They may express their feelings in words, or they may use nonverbal cues to show emotion. In fact, nonverbal cues—gestures, facial expressions, and tone of voice—may be more accurate indicators of a person's true feelings than verbal expressions. For example, the characters in "Scissors" unconsciously express their true feelings nonverbally because they are not free to give verbal expression to what they are thinking.

2. Divide the story into sections and students into groups. Assign each group a different section of the story, and ask group members to find, list, and interpret the meaning of all the nonverbal cues in their section of the story. Use the following examples from the first page of "Scissors" as a model:

   • Harold drops his paper when Louise and Robbie enter the shop: Harold is taken by surprise.

   • Louise kisses Harold on the cheek: She feels affection for him and knows him well.

3. Have each group report its findings to the class.

WRITING

The following assignments may be done in or out of class. **B** designates an assignment suitable for beginning writers; **I**, intermediate writers; **E**, more experienced writers. (Assignments that appear in the student anthology are in regular typeface. Additional assignments, which appear only in this teacher's guide, are in italics.)

B Though Harold and Louise loved each other, personality differences pulled them apart. What do you think they said to each other when they broke up? Write a conversation in which they discuss their differences.

I Harold and Louise were in school together. Based on their personalities as adults, imagine what they were like as teenagers. Write a brief description that might have appeared next to each one's picture in their high school yearbook. What kind of personality did each have? What clubs or organizations did each belong to? What were each person's plans for the future?

E The story is told by an outsider—an unnamed person who doesn't participate in the action. Imagine how the story would change if it were told by Louise's husband. Write the story of Louise and Harold's relationship from George's point of view. If you want, use the following beginning to get started.

"Louise and Harold think that I don't know about their past relationship, but I know all about it. I first found out when . . ."

E *What is Louise like? What is Harold like? Compare and contrast their personalities.*

UNFOLDING BUD

(PAGES 62-63)

· ·

POEM SUMMARY

A speaker compares a water lily's blossoming to the gradual blossoming of a poem. At first glance, the poem seems "tight-closed," but on subsequent readings, it slowly opens to reveal its beauty and meaning.

· ·

STEP-BY-STEP LESSON PLAN

1. Ask the pre-reading question:

   • Has your understanding of a poem ever changed over several readings?

Start a discussion by talking about a time when your understanding of a poem deepened after you read it several times. Ask students what kinds of poems they like and why. Do they enjoy poetry that rhymes or has a marked rhythm? If the class has had little experience with poetry, read several short poems aloud to them, choosing poems that are very different from one another in content and form. Ask students which they liked best and why.

2. Many people have never seen a water lily. To help set the stage for "Unfolding Bud," show students pictures of the flower. (Monet's *Water-Lily Pool* is frequently anthologized and therefore easy to find.)

3. Read the purpose statement aloud to help students set a goal for reading:

   • As you read, compare your experience reading poetry with the poet's.

4. Give students time to read the poem silently, or ask a student to read the poem aloud.

5. Ask the following literal **L**, interpretive **I**, and critical **C** reading questions. (Questions that appear in the student anthology are in regular typeface. Additional questions, which appear only in this teacher's guide, are in italics.)

L What natural event is described in the first stanza, or part, of the poem? Why does the speaker describe the event as "amazing"?

Answer: The speaker is describing the blossoming of a water-lily bud into a flower. The event is amazing to the speaker because the bud is transformed into a thing of great beauty.

L What comparison is made in the second stanza? In the third?

Answer: In the second stanza, the poet compares a hastily read poem to a tightly closed bud. In the third stanza, the poet compares the gradual revelation of a poem's beauty and meaning over several readings to the gradual blossoming of a bud into a beautiful flower.

I Do you think the comparisons are effective? Why or why not?

Answer: Students' answers will vary. It's likely that some students will object to the idea that a poem should reveal itself slowly through more than one reading. Others may question whether "Unfolding Bud" itself works in that way.

C *The first line of each stanza is similar. What purpose does the similarity serve?*

Answer: The similarity among the lines ("One is amazed," "One is not amazed," "Yet one is surprised") establishes a pattern and helps readers follow the comparison. The first line of stanza 2 and the first line of stanza 3 act as transitions.

6. End the lesson with activities that meet students' needs, interests, and learning goals.

· ·

ACTIVITIES

LITERATURE

Similes and Metaphors

1. Point out to students that "Unfolding Bud" is built around a simile and a metaphor. Define *metaphor* as a comparison that illustrates a similarity between two people, places, or things. Explain that unlike a simile, which is signaled by the use of the word *like*, *than*, or *as*, a metaphor is an indirect comparison. (For a more detailed description of similes, see page 83 of this *Teacher's Guide*.) Clarify the difference between the two types of comparisons by writing the following paraphrases of sections of the poem on a chalkboard:

   - *simile*: One is not amazed by a poem, which is *as* tight-closed *as* a tiny bud.

   - *metaphor*: One is amazed by a water-lily bud unfolding, taking on a richer color and new dimensions. One is surprised to see a poem gradually unfolding, revealing its rich inner self.

2. Ask students to think of other "unfolding" comparisons. For example, the gradual unfolding of the meaning of a poem might be compared to the gradual rising of the sun. Or ask students to create new comparisons to describe familiar things—a very hot (or cold) day, a lovely smile, a flashy car. Encourage students to be playful and creative.

3. After students have composed several similes or metaphors, discuss how these types of comparisons help readers understand and picture ideas.

COMMUNICATION

Reading Before a Group

1. Have each student select a poem to read aloud from *Expressions* volumes 1 or 2 or from another book.

2. Make sure that each student practices reading his or her poem aloud, alone or with a partner. Students should experiment with the volume and tone of their voices and with the emphasis placed on individual words.

3. Have each student read the poem he or she has chosen to the class.

WRITING

The following assignments may be done in or out of class. **B** designates an assignment suitable for beginning writers; **I**, intermediate writers; **E**, more experienced writers. (Assignments that appear in the student anthology are in regular typeface. Additional assignments, which appear only in this teacher's guide, are in italics.)

B Imagine that you are in charge of choosing poems for a new book. Would you include "Unfolding Bud"? Write a note explaining why you would—or wouldn't—put the poem in your book.

B *Write a three-stanza poem of your own, following the format of "Unfolding Bud." Use your imagination to compare one event or process to another. Use the following as the first lines of your three stanzas:*

   - *"One is amazed by . . ."*

   - *"One is not amazed, at first glance, by . . ."*

   - *"Yet one is surprised to see . . ."*

I The speaker in the poem is amazed by a small, everyday event. Write about a common event that amazes you.

E Just as someone's understanding of a poem can deepen, so can someone's understanding of another person. Write about a time when your first impression of someone changed as you got to know the person better.

THE RIGHT KIND OF HOUSE
(PAGES 65-77)

. . . .

STORY SUMMARY

When Mr. Waterbury arrives in Ivy Corners looking for a house to buy, the only one that interests him belongs to an elderly woman, Sadie Grimes. The house is for sale at a price several times what it's worth. Why is Mr. Waterbury willing to pay the price? The mystery is solved when Sadie Grimes tells him the tale of her son, a thief who was murdered by his accomplice for hiding from him a fortune in money they had stolen. Since her son's death, Sadie has sought vengeance on the accomplice, a man whom she has never seen. The high price on the house is a trap she has set to capture him: Only the accomplice would be willing to pay her price, because only the accomplice knows that the house contains stolen money. Mr. Waterbury is her man, and Sadie poisons him.

. . . .

STEP-BY-STEP LESSON PLAN

1. Ask the pre-reading questions:

   - Do you like mystery stories? When you watch a mystery unfolding in a movie or a TV show, do you try to solve it?

   Start a discussion by describing how people gather clues when they read or view a mystery story. Ask students to give specific examples from their own experience.

2. Read the purpose statement aloud to help students set a goal for reading:

   - As you read, ask yourself why [Mr. Waterbury] wants the house so much—and why the owner has set the price so high.

3. Have students take turns reading the story aloud. Ask the rest of the class members to follow along in their books, listening carefully for potential clues that might solve the mystery of the high price. Each time a clue is read, students should say "Stop!" to the reader. List clues on a chalkboard.

4. Ask the following literal **L**, interpretive **I**, and critical **C** reading questions. (Questions that appear in the student anthology are in regular typeface. Additional questions, which appear only in this teacher's guide, are in italics.)

L According to Mr. Hacker, the real estate man, why is Sadie Grimes asking such a high price for her run-down old house? What is the *real* reason?

Answer: Mr. Hacker believes Sadie is so sentimental about the house that she has put a ridiculously high price on it to prevent its being sold. However, the high price is actually a trap to catch her son's murderer.

L Though Sadie Grimes and the other people in Ivy Corners don't know it, Mr. Waterbury once knew Sadie's son. Describe Michael Grimes and Mr. Waterbury's secret past.

Answer: The two men were partners in crime. Mr. Waterbury shot Michael to death for double-crossing him and trying to avoid sharing a large sum of money they had stolen together.

L Why is Mr. Waterbury willing to pay such a high price for Sadie Grimes's run-down old house?

Answer: He knows that Michael hid the stolen money in the house.

I What do you think will happen to Mr. Waterbury? To Sadie Grimes?

Answer: Students' answers will vary. One likely scenario is that Mr. Waterbury dies of poisoning and that Sadie Grimes, being an elderly and sympathetic figure, is not punished for the crime.

I In your opinion, is "The Right Kind of House" a mystery story, a revenge tale, or both? Explain why you feel as you do.

Answer: Students' answers will vary. Arguments can be made for either point of view, but the organization of the plot suggests a mystery rather than a revenge tale, which usually begins by showing the avenger grievously wronged. Students might enjoy contrasting the organization of plot events in "$100 and Nothing!" (a revenge tale on pages 99–109 of the student anthology) and "The Right Kind of House."

C *Review the story in your mind. What details and events are, on second look, unlikely to occur or unbelievable? Did these details and events strike you as implausible the first time you read the story? If not, why not?*

Answer: Students may mention the following details and events as unlikely or unbelievable: that a real estate agent in a small town like Ivy Corners would be unaware of the nature of Michael Grimes's death—or would list a house for five years at a price three times what it's worth; that Sadie Grimes never knew what her son did for a living during the nine years he was away from home, never saw his accomplice even though he was in her home, and, despite her modest income, never searched for and found the money. It's likely that students accepted all plot details at face value during their first reading of the story; most readers are so intent on discovering the resolution to the mystery that they do not notice implausibilities.

5. End the lesson with activities that meet students' needs, interests, and learning goals.

· ·

ACTIVITIES

LITERATURE

Plot and Characterization

1. Explain to students that the main feature of "The Right Kind of House" is its plot, which is designed to lead up to a surprise ending. Because the author wants readers' attention focused on the plot, he provides very little information about the characters.

2. Ask students to reread the story, listing all the details that are provided about each of the main characters—Aaron Hacker, Mr. Waterbury, and Sadie Grimes. Students should notice that these are one-dimensional, flat characters. (For a more detailed description of flat characters, see page 101 of this *Teacher's Guide.*)

3. Ask students why the author provided so little description of the characters. Students should see that if the characters were presented in a fuller, more rounded way, they might begin to seem real, and the darkly humorous tone of the story— particularly the poisoning—would seem inappropriate.

COMMUNICATION

Stereotyping

1. Point out to students that the characters in "The Right Kind of House" are stereotypes. (Aaron Hacker is the talkative small-town businessman. Sally hearkens back to an old stereotype of a secretary—the gum-chewing incompetent. Sadie is the white-haired grandmother in a cardigan sweater.)

2. Ask students how they feel about the use of stereotypes in the story. It's likely that students didn't notice or care because they were focusing on the mystery rather than the characters.

3. Discuss how stereotyping can be harmful. Have students collect examples of stereotypical thinking they encounter in their daily lives and on TV. Ask:

   • Where do these stereotypes originate? What can be done to combat them?

WRITING

The following assignments may be done in or out of class. **B** designates an assignment suitable for beginning writers; **I**, intermediate writers; **E**, more experienced writers. (Assignments that appear in the student anthology are in regular typeface. Additional assignments, which appear only in this teacher's guide, are in italics.)

B Imagine that you are making a movie based on "The Right Kind of House." What actors would you hire to play the following roles? Give reasons for each of your choices.

   • Aaron Hacker

   • Sally the secretary

   • Sadie Grimes

   • Mr. Waterbury

I Imagine that you are selling your house or renting the apartment you live in. Write an ad that makes the place sound as attractive as possible. (Stick to the facts, but make them appealing.) Then describe the place in a way that would keep anyone from wanting to buy it.

E The last lines of "The Right Kind of House" are as follows:

   Waterbury put down the empty glass and licked his lips, his eyes no longer focusing, his head rolling loosely on his shoulders.

   "Ugh!" he said. "This lemonade is bitter."

What happened just after the point where the story ends? Write a new ending that picks up where the present one leaves off.

E *Write a plot summary of the story. Include only those details and events that people who haven't read the story would need to understand it.*

OLD COUPLE

(PAGES 78-79)

· ·

POEM SUMMARY

A speaker observes an elderly man and woman peering apprehensively out of their apartment window. He imagines the fears that they must feel—fear for their safety, fear of losing their home, fear of hunger, fear of illness.

· ·

STEP-BY-STEP LESSON PLAN

1. Ask the pre-reading question:

   • Have you ever felt frightened when you were home alone at night?

To start a discussion, describe a time when you were alone and afraid. Ask students to share their experiences with fear. Talk about the difficulty of overcoming it, even when you know it is irrational.

2. Read the purpose statement aloud to help students set a goal for reading:

   • As you read the poem . . . , try to imagine what it's like to be old and weak and lonely—and to feel . . . fear all the time.

3. Give students time to read the poem silently, or ask a student to read the poem aloud.

4. Ask the following literal **L**, interpretive **I**, and critical **C** reading questions. (Questions that appear in the student anthology are in regular typeface. Additional questions, which appear only in this teacher's guide, are in italics.)

L What is the old couple afraid of? Do you think the fears are reasonable?

Answer: The couple is afraid of being murdered, of being evicted, of having nothing to eat, of painful illness. Students will probably disagree about whether the fears are reasonable. Responses will depend upon students' interpretation of the old couple's environment and financial status.

I *Who do you think is the speaker in the poem—the "I" in lines 4, 13, and 15? Where do you think he or she watches the old couple from? In your opinion, can the speaker really know what the couple fears? How?*

Answer: Students may assign various identities to the speaker—neighbor, friend, police officer, social worker, possibly even thief. The speaker may be either on the street or in a neighboring building but must be close enough to see the old man get up to lower his shade. The speaker may have spoken with the old man and woman and therefore know what they fear, or he or she may simply be guessing.

I Why does the old couple watch the street? What might the husband and wife be watching for?

Answer: Students may offer a variety of reasons. The husband and wife may have nothing else to occupy their time except watching whatever happens outside their window. They may be watching for someone coming to visit them. Or they may also be watching for danger.

I Why does the old man keep his wife from turning on the lights?

Answer: Students may offer several explanations. The old man may be trying to save electricity. He may fear people seeing into the apartment. Or he may just want to hold her hand for comfort and companionship.

I What emotion do you feel most strongly when you read the poem? What do you think the speaker is feeling?

Answer: Students' answers will vary, but most students will probably say that they feel fear, sadness, or pity. The speaker probably experiences similar feelings.

C *Why does the poem include a brief description of the weather?*

Answer: The gloomy weather symbolizes the harshness of the urban world and emphasizes the dreariness of the old couple's life. (Other answers are possible.)

5. End the lesson with activities that meet students' needs, interests, and learning goals.

··························

ACTIVITIES

LITERATURE

Tone

1. Explain to students that *tone* refers to a writer's attitude about what he or she is saying. Introduce the concept of tone in literature by linking it to tone of voice.

2. Write the following sentence on a chalkboard:

   • "I'm so sorry that I can't make it to your party tomorrow."

Ask several students to read the sentence aloud, each expressing a different attitude, such as sarcasm, regret, or defensiveness. Discuss how tone of voice affects how a message is perceived.

3. Tell students that tone in writing is communicated through such elements as word choice and imagery.

4. List the following descriptions on a chalkboard:

   • menacing

   • compassionate

   • cold and uncaring

Ask students which word or words best describe the tone of "Old Couple." Have students support their interpretations by reading the poem (or sections of it) in the appropriate tone of voice. Make sure that students analyze the use of specific words and imagery from the poem when discussing its tone.

COMMUNICATION

Ageism

1. Ask students to brainstorm words that describe elderly people. Encourage students to give their first, "unedited" responses. On a chalkboard, make a list of at least twenty words.

2. Together with students, analyze the list. Ask:

   • Do most of the words have positive or negative connotations (emotional associations)?

3. If most of the words have positive connotations, ask students to analyze the forces that have shaped their perceptions of the aged. If most of the words have negative connotations (a more likely outcome), discuss the problem of ageism, or discrimination against the elderly. Build a discussion around the following questions:

   • What are some of the forces that shape Amercans' perceptions of the elderly?

   • How does ageism affect the elderly's ability to get and hold good jobs? Receive first-rate medical treatment for life-threatening illnesses? Influence legislators?

   • What can be done to combat ageism?

WRITING

The following assignments may be done in or out of class. **B** designates an assignment suitable for beginning writers; **I**, intermediate writers; **E**, more experienced writers. (Assignments that appear in the student anthology are in regular typeface. Additional assignments, which appear only in this teacher's guide, are in italics.)

B Imagine that you are a TV reporter working on a special show about the problems of the elderly. Write a list of questions that you could use to interview the old couple in the poem.

B *Write a conversation that might take place between the speaker and the old couple. Have the two old people explain what they fear and why they fear it.*

I The old couple is afraid of many things. Describe one of your fears.

E Imagine that you live in the old couple's neighborhood. Write a letter to the editor of the local newspaper. Explain what you think should be done to make older people in the community feel safe.

GETTING THE FACTS OF LIFE
(PAGES 81-95)

STORY SUMMARY

When twelve-year-old Minerva offers to accompany her mother to the welfare office for the first time, she has no idea what the experience will be like. By the time they have completed their interview with a case worker and begun their walk home, Minerva has developed a new understanding of her mother and has taken a giant step toward adulthood.

STEP-BY-STEP LESSON PLAN

1. Ask the pre-reading question:

   • Have you ever been forced to swallow your pride in order to get the help you needed?

Start a discussion by asking students what they think is the hardest thing to ask for. Advice? Money? Help with a job? Something else? Have students describe times when they had to ask other people for help and how they felt.

2. Read the purpose statement aloud to help students set a goal for reading:

   • As you read, ask yourself what facts of life the title refers to.

3. Give students time to read the story silently, or ask them to take turns reading it aloud.

4. Ask the following literal **L**, interpretive **I**, and critical **C** reading questions. (Questions that appear in the student anthology are in regular typeface. Additional questions, which appear only in this teacher's guide, are in italics.)

L Why does Mrs. Blue want one of her children to go with her to the welfare office? Why does Minerva offer to go?

Answer: Mrs. Blue doesn't like to walk far without company. According to Minerva, an African-American woman alone feels exposed and threatened, particularly in white neighborhoods, and Mrs. Blue attracts attention in black neighborhoods because she is light-skinned and has straight hair. Minerva offers to go with her mother because she doesn't want to baby-sit her brothers and sisters.

I How does Minerva feel as she and her mother near the welfare office? Why does she feel this way?

Answer: Minerva feels frightened, embarrassed, and confused. Her feelings stem, in part, from her fear that someone she knows will see her and her mother walking into the office.

I *Why is Minerva surprised to see white people in the welfare office?*

Answer: Minerva seems to have had little contact with white people other than when she walks through a wealthy white neighborhood on her way to somewhere else. She may have overgeneralized and inferred on the basis of her limited experience that all white people are rich.

I Why does Mrs. Blue want Minerva to stay in the welfare office waiting room? Why doesn't Minerva obey her mother?

Answer: Mrs. Blue wants to avoid the embarrassment of having her daughter see her forced to answer the case worker's humiliating questions. Minerva disobeys her mother and follows the case worker's order to accompany Mrs. Blue because the case worker is, in the child's eyes, an intimidating and powerful authority figure. (Other answers are possible.)

I In your opinion, did the case worker at the welfare office treat Mrs. Blue fairly? Is there anything that you think the case worker should—or shouldn't—have done?

Answer: Students' answers will vary. Some students will feel that the woman was only doing her job. Others will feel that she lacked empathy and respect for Mrs. Blue, particularly when she asked Mrs. Blue if she planned to have more children.

C *Why is Mrs. Blue a fitting name for Minerva's mother?*

Answer: Minerva's mother is struggling to make the best of a difficult time in her and her family's life. Given their difficulties, the name Blue is appropriate.

C Why is "Getting the Facts of Life" a fitting title for the story?

Answer: The title "Getting the Facts of Life" foreshadows, or hints at, the two kinds of knowledge Minerva gains—the facts about human reproduction and the fact that life presents difficult problems.

5. End the lesson with activities that meet students' needs, interests, and learning goals.

••

ACTIVITIES

LITERATURE

Flat and Round Characters

1. Point out to students that stories may contain two major types of characters—flat and round. *Flat characters* are one-dimensional. They do not undergo any psychological changes as a result of their experiences, and their behavior is very predictable. Most characters in TV situation comedies are flat. *Round characters* are more fully developed. They may change as a result of their experiences and, like real human beings, are less predictable. Lead characters in TV dramas are often round.

2. To ensure that students understand the two types of characters, ask them to give examples of TV characters who fit each type.

3. Have students identify the flat and round characters in the story. Ask them to justify their choices. To differentiate between the two types, students should ask themselves the following question:

   • Did the character change, grow, or learn something as a result of his or her experiences? If the answer is "yes," the character is round.

COMMUNICATION

Language and Messages

1. Explain that the words a person chooses to express a message affect how it is interpreted and received. For example, if a speaker uses language that is unfamiliar to the listener, then the listener will have difficulty understanding the message and may perceive the speaker as arrogant, regardless of the speaker's intent. Ask students to give examples from their own experience of times when they couldn't understand an important message because of the language used to express it, such as a time when a doctor explained a medical problem in technical terms that they didn't know.

2. Have students reread the dialogue between Mrs. Blue and the case worker in "Getting the Facts of Life." Ask students to pay attention to the manner in which the case worker speaks—particularly her choice of words. Then ask:

   • How would you characterize the case worker's manner of speaking? Formal or informal? Friendly or unfriendly? Educated or uneducated?

   • What attitude does the case worker's word choice convey to Mrs. Blue?

   • Is this attitude intentional or unintentional?

Students should see that the case worker's bureaucratic jargon is off-putting and conveys a supercilious attitude. Ask students what the case worker should do to convey a more positive attitude.

WRITING

The following assignments may be done in or out of class. **B** designates an assignment suitable for beginning writers; **I**, intermediate writers; **E**, more experienced writers. (Assignments that appear in the student anthology are in regular typeface. Additional assignments, which appear only in this teacher's guide, are in italics.)

B What is Mrs. Blue like? Make a list of at least three words that describe her. After each word, name a time or times when she shows the quality. Use the following example as a model:

   • Courageous—Mrs. Blue is courageous when she answers the case worker's embarrassing questions to help her family. Also, she is courageous when she walks past the men standing in front of the poolroom and the hotel.

I Minerva and her mother grow closer as a result of their shared experience. Write about a time when you grew closer to a parent or other family member as a result of an experience you shared.

E How did Minerva feel after the trip to the welfare office? Imagine that you are Minerva, and write a page in your diary describing your trip and what you learned as a result of it.

E *The manner in which a character speaks—his or her tone of voice and choice of words—tells you a lot about the person. Think of a person you know well. Write a dialogue for you and the person. Try to convey what the person is like by describing his or her tone of voice and using language that the person would actually use.*

MY FATHER'S LEAVING
(PAGES 96-97)

. . . .

POEM SUMMARY

A son describes returning home to find his mother crying just after his father has moved out. When the mother catches the son in the act of writing to his father, she asks him to leave. The son reflects on how he felt later, when he ignored his mother's request to stay. (Note: "Separating," on pages 113-126 of the student anthology, is about a similar situation—a boy confronting the breakup of his parents' marriage. It would make a good companion piece to this poem.)

. . . .

STEP-BY-STEP LESSON PLAN

1. Ask the prereading question:

   • Have you ever found yourself caught in the middle between two people you love?

To start the discussion, ask students to describe how they felt when they were torn between two loved ones. List the emotions on the chalkboard. (Respect students' privacy in this discussion. Focus on their feelings, not on the circumstances or people involved.)

2. Read the purpose statement aloud to help students set a goal for reading:

   • As you read, think about how you would feel if you were in the son's place.

3. Give students time to read the poem silently, or ask a student to read the poem aloud.

4. Ask the following literal **L**, interpretive **I**, and critical **C** reading questions. (Questions that appear in the student anthology are in regular typeface. Additional questions, which appear only in this teacher's guide, are in italics.)

L At the beginning of the poem, the father has just left home. Why did he leave?

Answer: He has been seeing another woman.

I *In your opinion, is the father gone for good?*

Answer: Students' answers will vary. Some students will argue that the father will return because a wife and family exert a stronger pull than another woman. Others will argue that there is a feeling of finality in the way the speaker describes his house just after his father moved out.

I Why did the mother ask the son to leave when she saw the father's name on the note? Do you think she was being fair? Why or why not?

Answer: The mother is angry and hurt by the father's breach of trust. She feels further betrayed—and, perhaps, jealous—when her son wants to communicate with his father. It is likely that most students will feel the mother overreacted. However, students' opinions of the mother's actions will depend on how they interpret the circumstances behind the father's leaving.

I The son says that his mother's voice sounds like "a whisper to someone else." Why does her voice sound strange? Why can't the son feel the weight of her hand on his arm?

Answer: The mother's voice sounds strange because she has been crying and is very angry. The son does not feel the weight of her hand because at that moment he feels as distant from her as she does from him. (Other answers are possible.)

I Why does the son ignore the mother when she asks him to stay?

Answer: Students' answers will vary. Some students will feel that the son's motivation is anger—the boy undoubtedly felt rejected when his mother asked him to leave. Others will think that he is going out to look for his father. Still others may believe that the boy, suddenly thrust into the role of "man of the house," believes it is more manly to leave (like his father) than to stay.

C *Why might the poet have chosen to mention that the sun was shining and the grass had just been cut? What do these details add to the poem?*

Answer: The freshly mowed lawn (orderliness) and sunshine (hope and happiness) contrast sharply with the anger and upheaval that the family is experiencing. The contrast between the exterior and interior worlds creates irony.

5. End the lesson with activities that meet students' needs, interests, and learning goals.

ACTIVITIES

LITERATURE

Point of View

1. Define *point of view* as the perspective from which a poem or story is told. Point out to students that point of view has two aspects—physical (a speaker's proximity to the action) and psychological (a speaker's perceptions of the action).

2. Have students consider both aspects of the point of view of "My Father's Leaving." Ask:

   • What is the son's physical point of view of his parents' breakup?

   • What is his psychological point of view?

   • How do these two aspects of point of view affect the details included in the poem?

Students should see that the actions leading up to the parents' breakup occurred "offstage," where the speaker couldn't witness them. As a result, the poem begins with the son's discovery that the father has left—not the discussion between the parents or the father's walking out the door. Students should also understand how the psychological point of view affects the poem's content. To the speaker, what matters is the emotional aftermath of the father's leave-taking, not the physical act of leaving itself. As a result, the poem focuses on what happened immediately after the father walked out the door.

3. Have students analyze the psychological point of view of the second stanza. Ask:

   • From whose point of view is the incident told—the son's or the mother's?

   • How does this point of view affect whom you sympathize with?

4. Point out the shift in psychological point of view in stanza 3, when it becomes clear that the speaker is describing incidents that took place years before. Build a discussion around the following questions:

   • Why did the speaker leave home?

   • At the time, did he understand what motivated him to leave? Does he understand now, years later?

COMMUNICATION

Lack of Communication

1. Point out that the speaker and his mother had trouble communicating. Ask students to reread the poem looking for examples of lack of communication. They are as follows:

   • The mother and son don't speak of the other woman or the nights the father spent there.

   • The mother doesn't ask what—or why—the son is writing to his father.

   • The son doesn't say anything when his mother asks him to leave—or, later, to stay.

Ask students to analyze why, in each case, the speaker and his mother do not talk to each other. Students should see that the mother and son avoid talking about painful subjects.

2. Ask students to discuss the consequences of the mother and son's lack of communication. Have students describe similar situations in their own lives and how they opened communication.

WRITING

The following assignments may be done in or out of class. **B** designates an assignment suitable for beginning writers; **I**, intermediate writers; **E**, more experienced writers. (Assignments that appear in the student anthology are in regular typeface. Additional assignments, which appear only in this teacher's guide, are in italics.)

B What did the son write in the note to his father? Imagine you are the son, and write the note.

I What do you think happened after the end of the poem? Where did the speaker go? Did he return to his mother or go to live with his father? Imagine that you are the son, and write a page in your journal explaining where you went and how you felt.

I *Why did the mother and father in the poem split up? How did the breakup affect the family? Write about the cause and effects of the separation.*

E Write about a time when you were the son's age and you did something—even though you knew it was a mistake—because you wanted to feel grown-up and independent.

$100 AND NOTHING!
(PAGES 99-109)

....

STORY SUMMARY

A rural southern African-American woman describes the unhappy marriage of her friend Mary to the cruel and lazy Charles. He lets Mary support him and buy him expensive gifts but in return insults and belittles her. Mary bears Charles's abuse for a long time without complaint. But when she becomes terminally ill, she plots her revenge. After her death, she leaves Charles with just exactly what he asked for—"$100 and Nothing."

....

STEP-BY-STEP LESSON PLAN

1. Ask the pre-reading question:

   • Have you ever known someone who worked and sacrificed for an ungrateful loved one?

Start a discussion by asking students why someone might stay in an abusive or unsatisfying relationship.

2. Read the purpose statement aloud to help students set a goal for reading:

   • As you read, ask yourself how you would feel if you were Mary.

3. It's likely that some students will have difficulty reading and understanding the dialect in which the story is written. To overcome problems caused by the dialect, read the story aloud to them.

4. Ask the following literal **L**, interpretive **I**, and critical **C** reading questions. (Questions that appear in the student anthology are in regular typeface. Additional questions, which appear only in this teacher's guide, are in italics.)

L Where does Mary get the money to buy a house and open a store? What does this tell you about her?

Answer: Mary earns the money by selling vegetables from the acre of land she bought. Her success indicates that she is hardworking and intelligent.

I In your opinion, why did Mary marry Charles? Why did he marry her? Why did she continue to live with Charles even though he treated her so badly?

Answer: Mary probably married Charles because she felt lonely. Charles married for money. Mary probably stayed with Charles because she felt that having him to care for was better than being alone. In addition, Charles may have destroyed Mary's self-esteem to the extent that she believed that she didn't deserve better treatment.

I *The narrator believes that Charles was unkind to Mary because he was jealous of her business success. Do you think his mistreatment of Mary springs from jealousy? If not, what else might have motivated Charles to mistreat her?*

Answer: Students' answers will vary. Some students may argue that Mary's goodness made Charles feel guilty, which in turn made him angry. Other students may argue that Charles intended to drive Mary away so that he could have her house and store to himself.

I Why did Mary bring Maybelline home with her? Do you think Mary imagined Charles and Maybelline would get together? Did Mary look ahead and foresee how that relationship would turn out?

Answer: Students' answers will vary. Some students will believe that Mary brought Maybelline home with her simply because Mary needed help and wanted to leave the store to a relative. Other students will argue that Mary was plotting her revenge.

C Why did the writer choose to tell the story through Mary's friend rather than Mary herself?

Answer: The narrator's lively, informal manner of speaking lends a light tone to what is actually a very grim series of events. In addition, the resolution of the plot complications occurs after Mary's death.

5. End the lesson with activities that meet students' needs, interests, and learning goals.

....

ACTIVITIES

LITERATURE

Style

1. Define *style* as an author's manner of expression. Point out that word choice, sentence structure, and tone are three elements of an author's style.

2. Point out that the style of J. California Cooper— the writer of "$100 and Nothing!"—is very distinctive. Tell students that you're going to read aloud the first five paragraphs of the story. Direct them to listen and look for the three elements.

3. After you've read the excerpt, ask students to describe each element. List their responses on a chalkboard. Under the category of "word choice," students should notice the writer's use of slang (e.g., "right smart a money") and colloquialisms ("ever" for "every," "tention" for "attention"). Under "sentence structure," students should notice the frequent use of exclamations ("I seen something here was really something! Let me tell you!") and long, loose, conversational sentences ("Where we live is not a big town like some and not a little town like some, but somewhere in the middle, like a big little town."). Under the category of "tone," students should notice the writer's use of humor (". . . he had a mouth full of 'gimme' and a hand full of 'reach.' ")

4. Have students compare and contrast Cooper's style to that of other authors. To show similarity, you might have students reread the first few pages of Sandra Cisneros's "My *Tocaya*." To show contrast, ask students to reread the first few pages of Dan O'Brien's "Crossing Spider Creek."

COMMUNICATION

The Meaning of Gifts

1. Ask students to analyze why Mary gives gifts to Charles. In gratitude for his marrying her? As a way of making up for her "faults"? Other reasons?

2. Charles makes fun of the clothes Mary buys him as gifts and doesn't buy her any presents. Have students think about the meaning of Mary's choice of gifts to Charles and his failure to respond in kind. Ask:

   - What message does Mary send to Charles through her choice of gifts?

   - What message does Charles send to Mary by criticizing her gifts? By not buying any for her?

3. Analyze the meaning of gifts in general. Build a discussion around the following questions:

   - Why do people give each other gifts?

   - What messages might a person be sending when he or she gives someone a very expensive gift? A very inexpensive gift? A homemade gift?

   - What happens when two people exchange gifts of very different values—one very expensive, one very inexpensive?

   - Do you like selecting gifts for friends and family members? Why or why not?

WRITING

The following assignments may be done in or out of class. **B** designates an assignment suitable for beginning writers; **I**, intermediate writers; **E**, more experienced writers. (Assignments that appear in the student anthology are in regular typeface. Additional assignments, which appear only in this teacher's guide, are in italics.)

B Mary worked hard to build a successful business. Write about a time when you worked hard to achieve a goal. What was the goal? Did you achieve everything you set out to? How did you feel?

I Imagine that you are Mary's friend, and write a "Dear Abby" letter. Tell the advice columnist about your friend's problems, and ask her what you should do to help. Then imagine that you're Abby, and write back, giving your advice.

E Reread the last paragraph of the story. Do you think Charles has learned anything from his experience? Describe what you imagine he is thinking as he drives slowly away. What do you think will happen to him now?

E *Do you think Mary's revenge on Charles was fair? Did he deserve what happened to him? Did the punishment fit the crime? Explain your answers.*

THOSE WINTER SUNDAYS

(PAGES 110-111)

....

POEM SUMMARY

A speaker looks back at his childhood and describes how, on cold Sunday mornings, his father would rise early and build a fire so that the house would be warm when the rest of the family got out of bed. The speaker regrets that he never thanked his father for what he did for him. He realizes now, as he did not then, that love can be shown in small acts that are easily taken for granted.

....

STEP-BY-STEP LESSON PLAN

1. Ask the pre-reading question:

   ● How do parents express love for their children?

Start a discussion by describing ways that you show your children that you love them or that your parents showed love for you. Ask students to describe what they do to say "I love you" to their children.

2. Read the purpose statement aloud to help students set a goal for reading:

   ● As you read, notice the ways in which the father shows love for his son.

3. Give students time to read the poem silently, or ask a student to read the poem aloud.

4. Ask the following literal **L**, interpretive **I**, and critical **C** reading questions. (Questions that appear in the student anthology are in regular typeface. Additional questions, which appear only in this teacher's guide, are in italics.)

L The son says that no one ever thanked his father for getting up early and warming the house. Do you think the father expected to be thanked?

Answer: It seems as if the father did not expect to be thanked; otherwise, he would have made some comment or stopped getting up early to carry out this task.

I The first line of the poem says, "Sundays too my father got up early." What does the word *too* tell you about the father's habits? What other clues in the poem tell you about his life? Describe it.

Answer: The word *too* indicates that the father got up early every day. The description "cracked hands that ached / from labor in the weekday weather" indicates that the father worked outdoors in a physically demanding job. The phrase "chronic angers of that house" hints that the father was unhappy.

I Why does the son speak "indifferently" to his father? How do you think the father feels when the son speaks to him that way?

Answer: As a boy, the son speaks indifferently to his father because he fails to recognize how much his father does for him. The father may feel disappointed that his son doesn't recognize his acts of love. (Other answers are possible.)

I What does the son mean when he speaks of "fearing the chronic angers of that house"? Who do you think was angry? At what?

Answer: Apparently, the father or someone else in the house was frequently angry and made it unpleasant for the rest of the family. Since the father is the only other person mentioned in the poem, most students will feel the father is the one generating anger. Some students will believe that the father is angry with the son. Others may point out that polishing the son's shoes is an act of love, not aggression. Still others may feel that the father is angry at his lot in life rather than with a person.

C *Why does the poet repeat the phrase "What did I know" in the next to the last line of the poem?*

Answer: Repeating the line emphasizes the anguish and regret that the speaker is feeling.

I How old do you think the son was when the action of the poem took place? How old do you think he is now? Have his feelings for his father changed? How can you tell?

Answer: Students' answers may vary. Encourage students to support their answers with lines from the poem. Students should see that the last two lines of the poem indicate that the son's feelings have, indeed, changed over the years.

5. End the lesson with activities that meet students' needs, interests, and learning goals.

ACTIVITIES

LITERATURE

Imagery

1. Direct students' attention to the poet's use of "blueblack" to describe the early morning cold in the house. Ask what feeling the image, or word picture, suggests to the reader. (For a more detailed description of imagery, see page 79 of this *Teacher's Guide*.)

2. Explain to students that the description is an example of *synesthesia*—describing one type of sensory experience (in this case, tactile) as it might be perceived by a different sense (in this case, visual).

3. List the five senses on a chalkboard. Have students experiment with combining senses to create interesting and unusual imagery. Use the following as examples:

   - *sound / sight:* sunlight laughing on the stream

   - *sound / touch:* the echo of an absent loved one's touch

   - *touch / smell:* the stabbing odor of decayed meat

If students have difficulty getting started, ask the following questions:

   - If happiness were a color, what color would it be? Why?

   - If spring had a voice, how would it sound? How would autumn sound? Why?

   - If anger had an odor, what would it smell like? Why?

COMMUNICATION

Roles People Play

1. Define *role* as a set of behaviors a person is expected to display as a part of his or her job or other position. To clarify the definition, give students the following example: When playing professional football, a person is expected to be aggressive, demanding of himself and his teammates, and intolerant of mistakes. Off the field, when playing the role of a friend, the same person is expected to be supportive, forgiving, and patient.

2. Build a discussion about the role of father by asking the following questions:

   - What behaviors are expected of a good father nowadays?

   - What behaviors are expected of a successful businessman?

   - How might these behaviors conflict with the behaviors of the "good father" role?

   - How has the role of father changed over the past several decades?

   - Judging by today's standards, is the father in the poem a good parent?

   - Are you—or do you plan to be—the same kind of father as your father? Why or why not?

WRITING

The following assignments may be done in or out of class. **B** designates an assignment suitable for beginning writers; **I**, intermediate writers; **E**, more experienced writers. (Assignments that appear in the student anthology are in regular typeface. Additional assignments, which appear only in this teacher's guide, are in italics.)

B Family members often do things to help one another. Describe some small act of love that you regularly do or that someone does for you.

I "Actions speak louder than words." Would the father agree with this old saying? Would the son? Explain what you think the father and son would say.

E Looking back, the son says, "What did I know, what did I know." Imagine that you are he, and write a letter to the father. Tell him what you know now and how you learned it.

E *What were the "chronic angers" that the narrator mentions in the second stanza? Use your imagination, and describe who in the household was angry at what.*

SEPARATING

(PAGES 113-126)

· ·

STORY SUMMARY

Fourteen-year-old Michael is torn between his parents, who have been separated for four months. Michael's father has a girlfriend named Darilyn, and his mother has begun dating again. So it comes as a surprise to Michael when his father suddenly announces that he has decided to return home. When the father goes to tell the mother the news, he finds her preparing for a date. The father is taken aback to realize that he can't just pick up his old life where he left it. The parents begin to argue, and Michael loses his temper with both of them. The story ends with Michael's wishing silently to himself, "I wish I could change us." (Note: "My Father's Leaving," on pages 96–97 of the student anthology, is also about a boy confronting the breakup of his parents' marriage. It would make a good companion piece to this story.)

· ·

STEP-BY-STEP LESSON PLAN

1. Ask the pre-reading question:

   • When parents separate, who suffers more—the adults or the children?

To start a discussion, ask students to name some of the emotions two adults might feel when their marriage ends. List students' reponses on a chalkboard. Then ask students which of the emotions a child might feel. Follow up by asking what other emotions, if any, only a child would feel.

2. Read the purpose statement aloud to help students set a goal for reading:

   • As you read, try to understand how each family member feels about the breakup.

3. Give students time to read the story silently, or ask them to take turns reading the story aloud.

4. Ask the following literal **L**, interpretive **I**, and critical **C** reading questions. (Questions that appear in the student anthology are in regular typeface. Additional questions, which appear only in this teacher's guide, are in italics.)

L Whose choice was it that Michael's parents should separate? What were the reasons for the separation?

Answer: It was the choice of Michael's father, who says he wanted to leave because his wife made him feel older than his years and he felt as if things were closing in on him. He also says that his wife didn't turn out to be the person that he thought she was.

I How did Michael's mother feel about her husband during the first weeks of their separation? Have her feelings changed? How can you tell?

Answer: At first, Michael's mother felt angry and rejected. But by the evening on which the story takes place, her feelings have changed. She is sad, but she is also eager to get on with her life.

I What reason does Michael's father give for wanting to return home? Do you think this reason is the only one? Why or why not?

Answer: The father says he made a mistake but that it's over now and he wants to return home. Students may or may not believe that the stated reason is the only one. Many may argue that the real reason the father wants to return home is that his girlfriend, Darilyn, has returned to her husband.

I Children often get caught in the middle when their parents don't get along. In your opinion, is this happening to Michael? Explain.

Answer: Michael's discomfort at fulfilling the role of confidant for each of his parents and his angry speech to them near the end of the story indicate that he feels torn between them.

C *Why do you think the writer called the story "Separating" instead of "Separated" or some other completely different title?*

Answer: The writer may have wanted to emphasize that, even though Michael's father moved out four months earlier, all three characters are still in the midst of the process of separating—of finding out how to live apart from each other and start new lives. (Other answers are possible.)

5. End the lesson with activities that meet students' needs, interests, and learning goals.

· ·

ACTIVITIES

LITERATURE

Theme

1. Define *theme* as the central meaning of a story or poem. To introduce the concept of theme, read aloud to students an Aesop's fable, such as "The Boy Who Cried Wolf." Point out that while the theme of a fable is directly stated, the theme of a story or poem usually is implied.

2. Help students see the relationship between theme and conflict. (For a detailed description of conflict, see page 85 of this *Teacher's Guide.*) Explain that the major conflict of a story or poem—the problem that the main character is grappling with—is a clue to the theme. To illustrate this point, ask students to describe the central conflict of "The Boy Who Cried Wolf" (friction between a bored shepherd who cries "Wolf!" when there is none and his disgruntled neighbors who have been tricked by the prank). Point out that the resolution of the conflict (the neighbors' assuming that a genuine cry for help is phony and the subsequent destruction of the flock) leads to the theme (nobody believes a liar, even when he's telling the truth).

3. Ask students to state the theme of "Separating." Students' responses may vary but should account for the conflict between Michael and his parents. Possible statements of theme include the following:

- Children suffer the most when parents split up.

- The process of dissolving a marriage is a difficult one for both parents and children.

- Children inevitably become caught in the middle when their parents decide to separate.

COMMUNICATION

Effective Communication Checklist

1. The characters in "Separating" sometimes have difficulty communicating with each other. Open a discussion of ways to communicate effectively by listing the following techniques on a chalkboard. Have students copy the list and rate the importance of each item in achieving effective communication at home, in school, and on the job, by numbering from one (least important) to six (most important). Let students know that there are no right or wrong answers—just opinions based on experience.

- being a good listener

- noting nonverbal cues that indicate how someone is feeling

- expressing anger in a nonthreatening way

- criticizing in a nonjudgmental way

- being willing and able to express feelings honestly

- verifying your interpretation of a message (e.g., "You seem angry. Are you?")

2. Have students read and justify their ratings to one another. Record their answers on the chalkboard. In your role as discussion leader, make an effort to use relevant communication skills on the list.

3. After students have discussed the relative importance of each communication technique, ask them to evaluate how well they used the techniques in communicating with one another during the activity. Ask the following questions, making sure that students back up their answers with specific examples:

- Did you listen carefully to one another's opinions?

- Did you make note of nonverbal cues to how other people were feeling? For example, if someone looked eager to talk, did you make sure the person got a chance to?

- When you disagreed with someone, were you able to express your opinion without being judgmental or threatening?

- Did you make sure you truly understood what other people were saying?

WRITING

The following assignments may be done in or out of class. **B** designates an assignment suitable for beginning writers; **I**, intermediate writers; **E**, more experienced writers. (Assignments that appear in the student anthology are in regular typeface. Additional assignments, which appear only in this teacher's guide, are in italics.)

B Do you think that a man and woman no longer in love should stay together for the sake of their children? Explain.

I Imagine that the father in the story has asked you for advice. He wonders whether he should try to win back his wife or give up on the relationship. What would you tell him? Why?

E Will Michael's parents get back together? Explain what you think will happen to them.

E *What would the story be like if Michael's father told it? Rewrite the story from his point of view.*

THE BIRTHDAY
(PAGES 127-129)

······································

POEM SUMMARY

The speaker in this poem is celebrating her thirtieth birthday with her husband and son. As she prepares to blow out the candles on her cake, she thinks about what she might wish for. First, she thinks that she already has what she wants in her husband and son. Next, she thinks that perhaps she should wish for something unknown and unexpected to come into her life. Finally, she reflects that her life is a process of outgrowing the need to make wishes. The poem ends with her wishing that she could express her thoughts to her husband.

······································

STEP-BY-STEP LESSON PLAN

1. Ask the pre-reading questions:

   • When you were a child, what kinds of things did you wish for? Have the things you wish for changed as you have grown older?

To start a discussion, describe to students a childhood wish that you had that did or did not come true. Tell them about something you wish for now. Encourage students to talk about their wishes, past and present.

2. Read the purpose statement aloud to help students set a goal for reading:

   • As you read, compare your wishes with the speaker's. Ask yourself what exactly it is that she wishes she could tell her husband.

3. Give students time to read the poem silently, or ask a student to read the poem aloud.

4. Ask the following literal **L**, interpretive **I**, and critical **C** reading questions. (Questions that appear in the student anthology are in regular typeface. Additional questions, which appear only in this teacher's guide, are in italics.)

L How old is the woman in the poem? Why is this birthday often considered to be a special one?

Answer: The woman is thirty years old. A thirtieth birthday is often considered to be a milestone, the first "important" birthday since the twenty-first and a step toward genuine maturity.

I Why does the woman find it hard to make wishes? Does she believe this difficulty is harmful?

Answer: Students' answers will vary. Some students may argue that the speaker finds it hard to make wishes because she already has everything she wants in her husband and son. Others may feel that her difficulty stems from her age; "grown-ups" don't take wish making as seriously as youngsters. Students' interpretations of how the woman feels about her difficulty will depend upon whether they perceive the last stanzas as positive or negative.

I Is the woman satisfied with how her life has turned out so far? How can you tell?

Answer: Students' answers will vary. Some students will feel that the woman's comments in stanzas 3 and 4 about her husband and son indicate that she is satisfied with her life. Others may argue that her comments in stanza 6 indicate that she's not sure what she wants.

I *What does a person gain as he or she grows older? What does a person lose? Which are greater—the gains or the losses?*

Answer: Students' answers will vary. Among the gains that come with age are wisdom, maturity, experience, patience, the love of children and a mate, security, opportunities, responsibility, power or authority. Among the things lost with age are youthfulness, energy, optimism, parents' love and support, opportunities, freedom from responsibility.

I How would you define the difference between aging and maturing?

Answer: Students' definitions may vary but should distinguish between physical changes that come with the passing of time (aging) and psychological changes that come with the passing of time (growing more mature).

C *Paraphrase the meaning of the last five stanzas.*

Answer: The last five stanzas are likely to be the most difficult for students to understand. Here is one possible paraphrase: "I have seen women age / beautifully, with a / growing, luminous / sexuality:" (*Some women become more beautiful and sensual as they grow older.*) "now I know, each year / they've been slowly / stepping out of their wishes / like their clothes." (*Now that I, too, am growing older, I see that their beauty and sexuality stem, in part, from their lack of longing for things they don't have.*) "I stand here amazed / at what is happening to me, / how I've begun to lighten / of desires," (*I'm surprised to see that I, too, have begun to stop wishing* *for things I don't have.*) "getting down / to my secret skin, / the impossibly thin / membrane this side / of nothing." (*As I get older, I'm beginning to know and understand myself better, but I'm also inching my way toward death.*) "Husband, / I wish I could tell you." (*Husband, I wish I could articulate my feelings so that you could understand them.*)

I In your opinion, is the poem about growing older? Growing wiser? Both?

Answer: The poem is about growing wiser while growing older and reaching a better understanding of oneself and one's relation to others. (Other answers are possible.)

5. End the lesson with activities that meet students' needs, interests, and learning goals.

·····································

ACTIVITIES

LITERATURE

Similes, Metaphors, and Personification

1. Ask students to recall the definitions of simile and metaphor. (Simile is defined on page 83 of this *Teacher's Guide*; metaphor, page 95.)

2. Ask students to find and explain the metaphor in stanza 3 ("My husband and son *are* wishes") and the simile in stanza 8 ("stepping out of their wishes / like their clothes").

3. Define *personification* as giving human characteristics to nonhuman things.

4. Direct students' attention to the use of personification in stanza 6 ("darkness / so tall and handsome before me"). Explain to students that the speaker is giving human characteristics (the clichéd description of a very attractive man as "tall, dark, and handsome") to something nonhuman (the unknown possibilities in her life) to explain the attraction the unknown holds.

5. Have students use similes, metaphors, or personification to describe the items on the following list or on a list students generate themselves.

- a fast car
- messy hair
- a difficult task
- an uncomfortable chair
- a rude person

COMMUNICATION

Withholding Feelings / Expressing Feelings

1. Have students consider the meaning of the last two lines of "The Birthday." Ask:

- What keeps the speaker from telling her husband what she is thinking?

2. Ask students what the speaker in the poem might do to communicate her feelings to her husband. What could the husband do to help her? Have students form small groups and write a short dialogue between the speaker and her husband in which she tells him the thoughts and feelings in this poem. Write the following lines on a chalkboard to help students begin:

- *husband:* You had a funny look on your face just before you blew the candles out. What were you thinking?

- *wife:* I was thinking about how hard it is to know what I want.

3. Ask two students from each group to give a reading of the dialogue they have created.

WRITING

The following assignments may be done in or out of class. **B** designates an assignment suitable for beginning writers; **I**, intermediate writers; **E**, more experienced writers. (Assignments that appear in the student anthology are in regular typeface. Additional assignments, which appear only in this teacher's guide, are in italics.)

B What is your greatest wish for yourself? For your family? For the world? Make a wish list.

I Some families develop their own traditions for celebrating birthdays or other special occasions, such as holidays. Choose a special occasion, and describe how your family celebrates it.

I *Compare and contrast wishes you had as a child with wishes you have today.*

E Many folk stories and jokes are about someone who gets what he or she wants and then regrets it. Write about a time when you got what you wanted and later were sorry you did.

TWO KINDS

(PAGES 131-148)

STORY SUMMARY

In this chapter from *The Joy Luck Club*, Jing-mei Woo tells the story of her mother's failed attempts to make her into a child prodigy. Mrs. Woo arranges for Jing-mei to take piano lessons, but the girl makes no attempt to practice or learn. When Jing-mei performs for the first time in a talent show, she plays terribly. A few days after the show, Mrs. Woo stubbornly tries to force her to resume her music lessons. In the ensuing argument, the angry daughter says something that breaks the mother's determination forever. Many years later, following her mother's death, Jing-mei sits down at the piano and learns a lesson about herself, her mother, and her life.

STEP-BY-STEP LESSON PLAN

1. Ask the pre-reading question:

   • As a child, did you ever do something because your parents wanted you to? Perhaps you took music lessons or played a sport or joined an organization.

To start a discussion, describe a time when you felt forced by your parents to become involved in an activity. Encourage students to share their experiences.

2. Read the purpose statement aloud to help students set a goal for reading:

   • As you read, ask yourself, Why is the mother so determined to find a special talent in her daughter? Why is the daughter so determined not to develop it?

3. Give students time to read the story silently, or ask students to take turns reading the story aloud.

4. Ask the following literal **L**, interpretive **I**, and critical **C** reading questions. (Questions that appear in the student anthology are in regular typeface. Additional questions, which appear only in this teacher's guide, are in italics.)

I At the beginning of the story, the daughter says that she was excited about her mother's plans to make her a prodigy. What made her lose her enthusiasm later on?

Answer: The daughter expected to become a prodigy overnight and, as a result, win her mother's undying adoration. Once the daughter fails at her first few attempts, she becomes impatient with the notion of perfection and tired of disappointing her mother.

I How do you feel about the daughter's embarrassing experience at the talent show? Are you sorry for her, or do you think she deserved what happened to her? Why do you feel the way you do?

Answer: Some students will feel sorry for the child and reason that, because she was forced to take piano lessons against her will, she didn't deserve to be embarrassed. Others will argue that she needed to learn a hard lesson.

I Were you surprised that the mother wanted the daughter to continue taking piano lessons after the talent show? Why did the mother want the daughter to continue?

Answer: It's likely that most students were surprised that the mother didn't want the daughter to quit taking lessons after the disastrous performance. The mother may have wanted her daughter to continue taking lessons to teach her an important lesson about not giving up in the face of failure.

I Reread the last paragraph of the story. What is the meaning of the daughter's discovery? What has the daughter learned about herself?

Answer: On a literal level, the daughter discovers that the song she played for the recital, "Pleading Child," has a companion piece, "Perfectly Contented," and that each is one half of the same song. On a symbolic level, the adult daughter has come to terms with the "pleading child" she was and, as a result, feels the "other half of the song"—contentment.

I What does the title "Two Kinds" refer to? Do you think the title has more than one meaning? If so, what are they?

Answer: "Two Kinds" refers directly to the mother's statement that there are only two kinds of daughters—those who are obedient and those who follow their own mind. It may also refer to the two very different generations of Chinese women and to "Pleading Child" and "Contented Child."

C *"Two Kinds" is the daughter's version of events. How does the daughter's telling the story affect your perceptions of her? Of her mother? How would the story change if the mother told it?*

Answer: Students may relate more closely to the daughter than the mother because the story is told from the daughter's point of view. If the story were told by the mother, readers would have a clearer understanding of the mother's motivations and feelings and might therefore relate to her.

5. End the lesson with activities that meet students' needs, interests, and learning goals.

······································

ACTIVITIES

LITERATURE

Conflict

1. Review with students the meaning of internal and external conflict. (See page 85 of this *Teacher's Guide.*)

2. Ask students to describe the major conflict in "Two Kinds" and to tell whether it is internal or external. Students should see that the main conflict is external.

3. Ask students if either of the main characters shows any sign of suffering from internal conflict. Students should recognize that Mrs. Woo's conflict seems to be purely external; she is absolutely sure that she is doing the right thing. Her daughter, on the other hand, is different.

4. Ask students whether they think Jing-mei the adult resolved the internal conflict she felt as a child.

COMMUNICATION

Managing Conflict

1. Point out that many conflicts can be avoided or resolved when people understand each other.

2. Divide the class into two groups—one to represent Jing-mei and the other to represent her mother. Assign the first group to describe how Jing-mei views her mother and to list reasons why she defies her. The group that represents the mother should describe how she views Jing-mei and list reasons why she wants her daughter to become a prodigy. Have students ask themselves these questions:

   • What motivates my character? What are her values?

3. On a chalkboard, write "Mother" and "Daughter." As each group presents its conclusions, summarize them in key words under the proper heading.

4. Together with students, review the lists on the chalkboard. When students have a clear picture of the misunderstandings between the two characters, have them suggest on how Jing-mei and her mother could have avoided conflict. Ask:

   • What could the mother have done to make her daughter feel less pressured to be special?

   • What could the daughter have done to alter the perception that she was stubborn and disobedient?

WRITING

The following assignments may be done in or out of class. **B** designates an assignment suitable for beginning writers; **I**, intermediate writers; **E**, more experienced writers. (Assignments that appear in the student anthology are in regular typeface. Additional assignments, which appear only in this teacher's guide, are in italics.)

B In a turning point in the story, the daughter looks at herself in the mirror and decides to stop trying to do well on her mother's tests. Imagine that you are the daughter, and write a page in your diary explaining the decision.

I The daughter says her mother never spoke to her about the talent show. What did the mother think? Imagine that you are she, and write a letter to a close friend describing the show and your daughter's performance.

E As an adult, the daughter has a deeper understanding of her mother and their longstanding disagreements and struggles. Describe a serious disagreement that you had with a parent or other adult when you were a child. Then compare and contrast how you felt about the situation as a child with how you feel today. Now that you are older, do you think the adult was right? Explain.

E *Imagine that you are a newspaper critic, and write a review of the talent show in which Jing-mei took part. Briefly describe the other performances, and write a detailed review of the daughter's piano performance.*

Contemporary's Whole Language Series

VIEWPOINTS

NONFICTION SELECTIONS

VOLUME 2

SONS AND DAUGHTERS

(PAGES 1-27)

· ·

THEME SUMMARY

Each of the four readings is about the relationship between an older or adult child and a parent. Humorist Dave Barry ("Lost in America") turns serious as he tells how his father's death cast his mother adrift. Kartar Dhillon ("The Parrot's Beak") learns what her mother had done years earlier to give her a better life. Anthony Walton ("Friend or Father?") confesses that he is still learning lessons that his father tried to teach him years before. Elisavietta Ritchie ("In Search of Eels") is touched when the smoked fish she buys for her elderly father triggers happy memories.

· ·

STEP-BY-STEP LESSON PLAN

1. Ask the pre-reading questions:

   • How does the relationship between a parent and child change when the child becomes an adult? Has your relationship with a parent or guardian changed as you have become older? How do you think it might change in the future?

   To start a discussion, describe ways that your relationship with your parents has evolved over time.

2. Read the purpose statement aloud to help students set a goal for reading:

   • As you read, think about your experiences as a son or a daughter. How are they similar to the experiences of the writers in this unit? How are they different?

3. Read aloud the first piece ("Lost in America"), or have students take turns reading the piece aloud. Then review the purpose statement and assign the other three readings. As an alternative, assign each of the readings to a student or a group of students to present to the rest of the class.

4. To ensure that students understand the pieces, ask them to summarize the main idea of each reading orally or on paper. Then ask the following literal **L**, interpretive **I**, and critical **C** reading questions. (Questions that appear in the student anthology are in regular typeface. Additional questions, which appear only in this teacher's guide, are in italics.)

L What were some of the problems troubling the mother in "Lost in America"?

Answer: The mother had trouble accepting her husband's death and may have regretted selling the family home.

I *In your opinion, does a person have the right to take his or her life? Why or why not?*

Answer: Students' answers will vary.

L In "The Parrot's Beak," what did Kartar Dhillon's mother do to help ensure her daughters' happiness? How did Dhillon react when her mother told her what she had done? Why?

Answer: Kartar Dhillon's mother prevented her husband from arranging marriages for their daughters. Dhillon's reaction to the news—stunned silence and gratitude—reflects her growing understanding of and love for her mother.

I In "Friend or Father?" Anthony Walton's father sums up what he has learned from life in adages—brief statements of advice. What advice does he give his son? What does the advice say about the father as a person?

Answer: The adages are in italic type and appear throughout the article. The father's advice shows him to be a practical, down-to-earth person who values common sense and experience over formal education.

L What made Elisavietta Ritchie ("In Search of Eels") take her father on an outing? What memories did the smoked eel trigger in her mind?

Answer: Ritchie decided to take her father for a drive because he seemed lethargic and depressed. The smoked eel reminded Ritchie of a childhood outing, when her father bought smoked eel and she tasted it for the first time, and of a trip to Japan she and her parents took years later, when she was a teenager.

C Elisavietta Ritchie uses a lot of specific details in her writing. Find examples of description that appeals to each of the five senses.

Answer: The following are representative of her style: sight—billowing white curtains; smell—the fragrance of newly mowed grass; sound—the bellow of a freighter; taste—the smoky, salty taste of eel; touch—the father's "limp, resistant, heavy" body.

L Which readings show a parent acting as a traditional authority figure? Which show a child acting like a parent toward his or her parent?

Answer: The mother in "The Parrot's Beak" and the father in "Friend or Father?" behave like traditional, all-powerful authority figures, while the emotionally frail mother in "Lost in America" and physically frail father in "In Search of Eels" are, in some ways, childlike and dependent. As a result of the parents' failing health, the children assume parental roles.

I *What do you think each of the four writers in this unit would say if asked to describe his or her feelings about being a son or a daughter?*

Answer: Students' answers will vary.

5. End the lesson with activities that meet students' needs, interests, and learning goals.

· ·

ACTIVITIES

RHETORIC

Past and Present Time

1. Point out to students that none of the pieces in the Sons and Daughters unit is organized in *chronological order*, or time order.

2. Together with students, review the organization of "Lost in America." Students should see that Barry begins the piece with a present-time description of his drive to Essex, Connecticut, with his mother (note the present participles "are driving" and "are hoping") and then switches, in paragraph 2, to the recent past (note the present perfect "has been rootless"), ending the paragraph with a description of actions that occurred in the more distant past (note the past "sold" and past perfect "had lived in"). In the second half of the piece (page 4), Barry returns to present time and the visit he made to Essex with his mother and then briefly describes, in chronological order, pertinent events leading to his mother's death. The piece ends with a flashback. Ask:

- Why might Barry have decided to begin his story in the middle, with the drive to Essex, rather than at the beginning, with his father's death?

Students should see that, in typical newspaper style, Barry creates a strong *lead*, or beginning, by starting his story with a description of an incident that is likely to generate interest or curiosity.

3. Together, review the organization of the other three pieces.

COMMUNICATION

Self-Perception

1. Point out to students that two of the readings— "The Parrot's Beak" and "Friend or Father?"— revolve around parents who were critical of their children. Discuss with students the influence that parents have over their child's self-image.

2. Discuss ways that parents can help their children form positive self-images.

WRITING

The following assignments may be done in or out of class. **B** designates an assignment suitable for beginning writers; **I**, intermediate writers; **E**, more experienced writers. (Assignments that appear in the student anthology are in regular typeface. Additional assignments, which appear only in this teacher's guide, are in italics.)

B Write a note to a parent or guardian thanking the person for his or her help.

B *Choose one of the adages in "Friend or Father?" and explain what it means.*

I In "Friend or Father?" Anthony Walton describes lessons that he learned from his father. Describe a time when you learned a lesson in life from an older person.

E The taste of smoked eels brings back happy memories for Elisavietta Ritchie and her father in "In Search of Eels." Describe a food, aroma, piece of music, or other sensory experience that triggers happy memories in your mind. Begin by describing the sensory experience in the present; then flash back to the past, and describe the memory the experience triggers.

CAUGHT BETWEEN CULTURES

(PAGES 29-49)

. . . .

THEME SUMMARY

The four readings in this unit focus on people whose backgrounds force them to cope with two different cultures—their native cultures and mainstream United States culture. Centenarian Sarah Delany ("Around Brick Walls") describes with relish how she foiled the bureaucracy and became the first African-American teacher in an all-white high school. Andrea Martínez ("Fitting In") recalls the discrimination she suffered as a Zapotec Indian in Mexico and as a newcomer to the United States. Adam Hryniewicki ("Interview . . .") praises the United States as a land of opportunity but laments our "buy-now, pay-later" mentality. Lewis Sawaquat ("For My Indian Daughter") describes how he became interested in his Native-American roots.

. . . .

STEP-BY-STEP LESSON PLAN

1. Ask the pre-reading questions:

   ● What does the word *culture* mean to you? What would you say if someone asked you to describe the culture you live in?

Start a discussion by asking students to list customs, institutions, or beliefs that they think vary from culture to culture. Begin by listing the following on a chalkboard: *dating, marriage, education, food.*

2. Read the purpose statement aloud to help students set a goal for reading:

   ● As you read, put yourself in the place of the people being described. Ask yourself what you would have done in each situation.

3. Read aloud the first piece ("Around Brick Walls"), or have students take turns reading the piece aloud. Then review the purpose statement and assign the other three readings. As an alternative, assign each of the readings to a student or a group of students to present to the rest of the class.

4. To ensure that students understand the pieces, ask them to summarize the main idea of each reading orally or on paper. Then ask the following literal **L**, interpretive **I**, and critical **C** reading questions. (Questions that appear in the student anthology are in regular typeface. Additional questions, which appear only in this teacher's guide, are in italics.)

L How did Sarah Delany ("Around Brick Walls") trick the local board of education into hiring her?

Answer: Delany pretended there was a mix-up and skipped her face-to-face interview, sending a letter instead. Then she showed up for the first day of classes, too late for the board to transfer her.

L How does Delany feel about her African-American roots? The prejudice that has been directed at her?

Answer: Delany is proud of her heritage and "absolutely comfortable with" who she is. Though she has been the victim of prejudice, she has not become embittered by it.

L What difficulties has Andrea Martínez ("Fitting In") had to overcome?

Answer: In Mexico, as a Zapotec Indian and as a female, Martínez was discriminated against. She also has been discriminated against in the United States and has had to learn both Spanish and English to survive in her Mexican-American community.

L What does Adam Hryniewicki ("Interview . . .") like about life in the United States? Dislike?

Answer: Likes—the job opportunities, the control he has over his life, the chance to meet different people; dislikes—Americans' buying on credit

I Some people still view Native Americans as stereotypes rather than as individuals. In your opinion, what causes people to stereotype others? What effects have negative stereotypes of Native Americans had on Lewis Sawaquat ("For My Indian Daughter")?

Answer: Students are likely to mention a variety of causes. Negative stereotypes and hatred of Indians caused Sawaquat to lose touch with his roots.

I *Some Native-American groups have protested sports teams' use of Indian names and lore as insulting and sacrilegious. How do you feel about protests like these? How do you think the sports teams should respond? Why?*

Answer: Students' answers will vary.

C Sawaquat calls the second part of his article "Theft." What was stolen from him? Why does he give the name "Circle" to the last part of the article?

Answer: Sawaquat felt that his Native-American heritage had been stolen from him. The name "Circle" refers to "coming full circle" in at least three senses: Sawaquat's realization that other people's misconceptions about Indians were really no different from his own, his wish to pass his wisdom on to his daughter, and his harkening back in the conclusion of the article to the image used in the introduction—his daughter upstairs in her bed.

I Sarah Delany says, "Life is short, and it's up to you to make it sweet." How do you think Andrea Martínez, Adam Hryniewicki, and Lewis Sawaquat would respond to this statement?

Answer: Students' answers will vary.

5. End the lesson with activities that meet students' needs, interests, and learning goals.

· ·

ACTIVITIES

RHETORIC

Organization and Structure

1. Point out that Lewis Sawaquat chose to divide "For My Indian Daughter" into sections with subheads, or titles. Discuss the logic behind the breaks between sections and, if you haven't already done so, the titles. Help students see that the essay is structured around a basic pattern—*anecdote* (short story used to illustrate a point) plus summary of the meaning of the anecdote. Students should also note the circular structure of the essay. You might mention that the circle is a symbol of eternity and figures prominently in Indian art.

2. Point out the function of the subheads—to clue readers into the point, or significance, of each section of the article. Follow up by having students divide into sections a short piece, such as "Interview with Adam Hryniewicki." Ask them to write subheads for each section.

COMMUNICATION

Communication Barriers

1. Point out to students that the people in the four readings must overcome several different barriers, or obstacles, to communication. In the case of Andrea Martínez, for example, a major obstacle is language itself. When she first arrived here, she couldn't speak Spanish or English.

2. Ask students to describe communication barriers and ways to overcome them in each of the following cases:

   • Sarah Delany and the 1920s Board of Education

   • Andrea Martínez and her grandmother

   • the Zapotec Indians and the Mexicans

WRITING

The following assignments may be done in or out of class. **B** designates an assignment suitable for beginning writers; **I**, intermediate writers; **E**, more experienced writers. (Assignments that appear in the student anthology are in regular typeface. Additional assignments, which appear only in this teacher's guide, are in italics.)

B Adam Hryniewicki mentions things that he likes and dislikes about life in the United States. Which aspects of life in the United States do you especially appreciate? Which would you most like to change?

I Write about an incidence of prejudice that you saw or were a part of. What happened? How did you feel? If you could relive the situation, would you react the same way?

E Put yourself in the place of Lewis Sawaquat. Would you want your daughter to identify herself as Native American? Or would you avoid teaching her about her roots to help her more easily fit in with the mainstream? Explain.

E *The Delany sisters disagree about how to handle bigots. Sarah stayed on good terms with her racist "fair-weather friend," while Bessie says, "I wouldn't have had nothing more to do with her this side of Glory!" Who's right? Why?*

ACTS OF KINDNESS AND LOVE
(PAGES 51-73)

· ·

THEME SUMMARY

The four readings focus on unselfish acts. Sarah Meyers's loving letter to her dead grandfather ("Above and Beyond") is answered with an equally loving letter from a stranger. Molly Fulghum's present to her father ("The Good Stuff") leads to a deeper understanding between them. An old woman's generosity and thoughtfulness ("Grandma Hattie") cause Tom Bodett to write a loving tribute to her. The garden and bridge that Fred Chappell's father builds for his wife ("The Overspill") give their son insight into the power of love.

· ·

STEP-BY-STEP LESSON PLAN

1. Ask the pre-reading questions:

   • Think about the best gift you've ever given or received—not the most expensive, but the one that counted the most. What was the gift? What made it so special? Wasn't it that it showed how much you cared about someone or how much someone cared about you?

   Start a discussion by describing an act of kindness or love that touched you recently.

2. Read the purpose statement aloud to help students set a goal for reading:

   • As you read, think about the people in each of the readings. Imagine what motivated them to be so unselfish—and what results their acts of kindness and love produced.

3. Read aloud the first piece ("Above and Beyond"), or have students take turns reading the piece aloud. Then review the purpose statement and assign the other three readings. As an alternative, assign each of the readings to a student or a group of students to present to the rest of the class.

4. To ensure that students understand the pieces, ask them to summarize the main idea of each reading orally or on paper. Then ask the following literal **L**, interpretive **I**, and critical **C** reading questions. (Questions that appear in the student anthology are in regular typeface. Additional questions, which appear only in this teacher's guide, are in italics.)

I Why do you think Donald Kopp took the time to write to Sarah Meyers ("Above and Beyond")? How do you think she felt when she received his letter?

Answer: Kopp was touched by Meyers's letter and may have imagined how his grandchildren would feel in similar circumstances. Kopp's letter was probably a comfort to Meyers.

I What meaning did the items in the bag have for Molly Fulghum ("The Good Stuff")? For her father?

Answer: The items were favorites of Molly's and meant a lot to her. Knowing they were safe and at hand may have given her a sense of security. At first, her father did not understand the significance of the items. Later, he came to see that they were important.

L What acts of kindness and love are described in "Grandma Hattie"?

Answer: The grandmother sends money and cards to family members on special occasions; during the Depression, she went out of her way to feed hoboes.

C *Why does Tom Bodett's mother always stop telling the story of Grandma and the hoboes before explaining whether any hoboes came to the door?*

Answer: For both Bodett and his mother, the point of the story is to illustrate Grandma Hattie's unselfishness. As such, what matters to them is the gesture—not whether someone took her up on it.

I Describe the relationship between the father and son in "The Overspill." What kind of relationship do you think the father had with the mother?

Answer: Chappell and his father seem to have had a close and loving relationship. They enjoyed each other's company, spent free time together, and shared a secret joke. The father also seems to have had a loving relationship with his wife.

I How is Grandma Hattie's unselfishness toward the homeless different from the acts of kindness and love in the other three readings?

Answer: In the other readings, the acts were performed for one particular person. Grandma Hattie extended her kindness to anyone passing by her gate who needed help.

I *In each reading, an act of kindness results in a similar act by someone else. Identify the original and reciprocal act of kindness in each reading.*

Answer: Sarah Meyers's sending a loving letter to her grandfather brought Donald Kopp's kind and thoughtful response. Molly Fulghum's present of her "good stuff" and her father's realization of its true value led to the janitor's helping retrieve the items from the garbage. Grandma Hattie's acts of generosity caused Tom Bodett to write a loving story about her. The garden and bridge that Fred Chappell and his father built gave Chappell insight into the power of love and led to his writing a moving story.

5. End the lesson with activities that meet students' needs, interests, and learning goals.

· ·

ACTIVITIES

RHETORIC

Style

1. Define *style* as an author's means of expression. Ask students to contrast the styles of Fred Chappell and Tom Bodett. Explain that you're going to read aloud the first eight paragraphs of "The Overspill." Direct students to listen and look for three elements of style—use of description, word choice, and sentence length.

2. After you've read the excerpt, ask students to describe each element. List their responses on a chalkboard. Under the category of "use of description," students should note Chappell's detailed descriptions of sensory experiences (e.g., "Best of all was the firing, the clear yellow flame and the sizzle and snap of the vine-ribs and thorns, and the thin black smoke rising above the new-green willows. The delicious smell of it"). Under the category of "word choice," students should note that Chappell's diction is rather formal and sophisticated. You might point to some of the words that are glossed. Under the category of "sentence length," students should note that, on the whole, Chappell's sentences are long.

3. Read aloud the first five paragraphs of "Grandma Hattie," and have students contrast Bodett's style with Chappell's.

COMMUNICATION

Varying Perceptions

1. Point out that people may interpret the same things very differently. For example, the father and daughter in "The Good Stuff" at first have very different views about the paper sack.

2. Ask students to compare and contrast the perceptions of the following pairs of people about the situation or event described.

Situation	*People*
• sending a letter to heaven by balloon	Sarah / her mother
• filling a bag with treasures	Molly as a child / Molly as an adult
• Grandma Hattie's marking her fence	Hattie's neighbors / the hoboes
• the opening of the floodgates	the Chappell family / the paper company

WRITING

The following assignments may be done in or out of class. **B** designates an assignment suitable for beginning writers; **I**, intermediate writers; **E**, more experienced writers. (Assignments that appear in the student anthology are in regular typeface. Additional assignments, which appear only in this teacher's guide, are in italics.)

B If you were to put together a bag of items you treasure, what would go into it? Why?

I Describe an act of kindness that touched you.

E Bob Greene is known for writing human-interest stories. Rather than just reporting facts, this type of story shows how people think, feel, and act. Imagine that you are a newspaper reporter, and write a human-interest story about the events in "The Overspill." Describe what happened, and interview the people involved.

E *Poet John Donne once wrote, "No man is an island." Explain what the statement means, using one of the readings in the unit as an example.*

WHERE DID IT COME FROM?

(PAGES 75-89)

....

THEME SUMMARY

Each of the four readings describes the invention or origin of a common object or product. The shopping cart was invented by Sylvan Goldman, a grocery-store owner who wanted shoppers to buy more items · when they visited his store. The type of gum we chew today was invented in 1870 by Charles Adams, who was looking for a substitute for rubber. Velcro fasteners were created by Swiss inventor George de Mestral, who found a way to make synthetic hooks akin to those he observed in nature. Coca-Cola ("Dr. Pemberton's Pick-Me-Up") was created in 1886 by John Pemberton, an Atlanta druggist.

....

STEP-BY-STEP LESSON PLAN

1. Ask the pre-reading question:

   • Have you ever looked at some common, everyday object—like a paper clip or a felt-tip pen—and said to yourself, Hmm . . . I wonder who thought that up?

Start a discussion by asking students to briefly relate the history of a famous invention.

2. Read the purpose statement aloud to help students set a goal for reading:

   • As you read each piece, think about how your life would be different if the product had not been invented. Ask yourself, In what ways is the discovery or creation of this invention like the others? In what ways is it different? Was the invention created by accident, or was it planned and developed over time?

3. Read aloud the first piece ("The Shopping Cart"), or have students take turns reading the piece aloud. Then review the purpose statement and assign the other three readings. As an alternative, assign each of the readings to a student or a group of students to present to the rest of the class.

4. To ensure that students understand the pieces, ask them to summarize the main idea of each reading orally or on paper. Then ask the following literal **L**, interpretive **I**, and critical **C** reading questions. (Questions that appear in the student anthology are in regular typeface. Additional questions, which appear only in this teacher's guide, are in italics.)

I Why do you think shoppers at first hesitated to use Sylvan Goldman's shopping carts? What made shoppers change their minds?

Answer: Since people were used to bringing their own shopping baskets from home, they may have felt that there was no use in buying more than they could carry home in their basket. Goldman's employees' wives disguised as shoppers helped persuade people to use the carts.

I *Cockleburs have been around for centuries. Why wasn't Velcro invented until the 1950s?*

Answer: Before the invention of the microscope, no one could have seen the tiny hooks that made cockleburs stick to clothing. And until fairly recently, the technology to manufacture fabric with microscopic hooks and loops in it did not exist.

C Why does the author of "Dr. Pemberton's Pick-Me-Up" keep the name of the product a secret until the last line of the story? Would you have enjoyed the article more if you had known from the start that it was about Coca-Cola? Why or why not?

Answer: Aurandt creates suspense by withholding the name of the product. Students' opinions about the effectiveness of the technique will vary.

L Which of the four inventions were the result of planning? Which were accidents?

Answer: Sylvan Goldman's shopping cart is the only invention that was completely planned.

I In your opinion, which of the four inventions described in this unit has had the most far-reaching effects?

Answer: Students' answers will vary. Encourage students to brainstorm less apparent but far-reaching effects of each invention, such as the number of jobs created by the manufacture of a product.

5. End the lesson with activities that meet students' needs, interests, and learning goals.

ACTIVITIES

RHETORIC

Development of Ideas

1. Point out to students that writers may *develop*, or support, their ideas in a variety of ways. List and give an example of each of the following techniques: sensory description (details that appeal to the five senses)—"chomping on wads of sap" ("Chewing Gum," page 79); facts and statistics—"The average supermarket loses 12 percent of its carts a year" ("The Shopping Cart," page 78); reasons—"According to some psychologists, one reason people chew more gum today is that they are more nervous than people of the past" ("Chewing Gum," page 81); examples—"Many doctors of the time . . . decided that the rubbery stuff was dangerous to health. For example, in 1869 one physician wrote an article warning that the chewing of gum 'would exhaust the salivary glands. . . .' " ("Chewing Gum," page 80).

2. Divide the class into four groups, one for each reading in this unit. Assign each group to look at its assigned piece for further examples of the four methods of development. (Warn students that all four methods may not be present in their piece.) Have each group report to the class as a whole.

COMMUNICATION

Problem Solving

1. Point out to students that invention is often a form of problem solving. For example, the shopping cart was invented to solve a problem—customers quit shopping when their baskets became too full.

2. Explain that it can be helpful to state a problem in the form of a question. For example, the above problem may be restated as follows: How can customers comfortably carry more items?

3. Divide the class into groups or pairs. Assign each team one of the following problems, or ask teams to think of problems they'd like to solve.

Problems

- long lines at the ticket office of a sports stadium

- trash and litter in a city park

- people marking trains with graffiti

4. Ask teams to think of different ways to state their problems; e.g.:

Problem: Traffic jams are occurring in the city between 6 and 9 A.M. and between 4 and 6 P.M.

Possible ways to state the problem as a question:

- How can we get people to arrive at and leave work at times other than rush hours?

- How can workers in the city get to their jobs without using their cars?

- How can we encourage people to carpool?

5. Ask each team to solve its assigned problem by answering the questions it generates, and have teams present their solutions to the class as a whole.

WRITING

The following assignments may be done in or out of class. **B** designates an assignment suitable for beginning writers; **I**, intermediate writers; **E**, more experienced writers. (Assignments that appear in the student anthology are in regular typeface. Additional assignments, which appear only in this teacher's guide, are in italics.)

B Imagine that you are a regular shopper at Sylvan Goldman's store in 1936. Write a letter to a friend in another town describing the new shopping carts and telling why you think they are a good—or a bad—idea.

I If you could invent something to make life easier or more fun, what would it be? Let your imagination go, and write a description of what your invention does and how it works.

E The design of the original shopping cart has changed very little over the years. Think of something that could be done to make the cart even more useful or easier to use. Write a description of your changes, and explain why shopping-cart makers should adopt your idea.

E There isn't much difference between one brand of chewing gum or soft drink and another; yet there are many different brands being successfully sold to the public. Make up a new brand of gum or soft drink, and write an ad for it. Tell people why your brand is unique or better than all the others.

E *Dramatize the accidental creation in Jacobs Pharmacy of the formula for Coca-Cola. Write dialogue and stage directions for the clerk and the customer.*

TURNING POINTS

(PAGES 91-107)

· ·

THEME SUMMARY

Each reading in this section describes a confrontation, decision, or event that changed the course of a person's life. When she was only six years old, Eula Lee Maddox ("Words in a Blue Notebook") stood up to a racist landowner. To cope with the death of her husband, Alice Lindberg Snyder ("Freedom") went to a therapist, who helped restore her sense of adventure and zest for living. Stand-up comic Louie Anderson ("And I Never Did") was a rebellious, overweight teenager who quit high school after an argument with his gym teacher. Penny Longworth ("Me and the Guy Upstairs") discovered new strengths and talents when she gathered the courage to leave her abusive husband.

· ·

STEP-BY-STEP LESSON PLAN

1. Ask the pre-reading question:

   • What important turning points have marked your life so far?

Start a discussion by describing a turning point in your own life.

2. Read the purpose statement aloud to help students set a goal for reading:

   • As you read, ask yourself, If this person had a chance to live life over, would he or she do things differently? What would this person's life be like if the turning point hadn't occurred?

3. Read aloud the first piece ("Words in a Blue Notebook"), or have students take turns reading the piece aloud. Then review the purpose statement and assign the other three readings. As an alternative, assign each of the readings to a student or a group of students to present to the rest of the class.

4. To ensure that students understand the pieces, ask them to summarize the main idea of each reading orally or on paper. Then ask the following literal **L**, interpretive **I**, and critical **C** reading questions. (Questions that appear in the student anthology are in regular typeface. Additional questions, which appear only in this teacher's guide, are in italics.)

L What turning point in the life of Eula Lee Maddox is described in "Words in a Blue Notebook"?

Answer: The reading focuses on Maddox's confrontation with a racist landowner.

I If you could use only one word to describe Maddox, what would it be? Why?

Answer: Students' answers will vary.

L What turning point in the life of Alice Lindberg Snyder does the reading "Freedom" describe?

Answer: The reading describes Snyder's decision to live life to the fullest regardless of her age.

I How do you feel about Snyder's decision to learn how to tap-dance despite being in her seventies? Why do you feel as you do?

Answer: Students' answers will vary.

I Do you think Louie Anderson ("And I Never Did") would have finished high school if he hadn't had such a bad experience in gym class? Why or why not?

Answer: Some students will feel that Anderson was too much of a rebel to have lasted much longer in school. Others may feel that a more understanding gym teacher—or other teacher—might have kept Anderson in school.

C *Louie Anderson wrote his autobiography entirely in the form of letters to his father. Do you think this was an effective method? What might be the advantages and disadvantages of this method?*

Answer: Some students will think the method is effective because they like the intimate, informal tone of Anderson's letter and are familiar and comfortable with the letter format. Others may feel that the letter format is too limited for a comprehensive autobiography.

I What is Penny Longworth's attitude toward life in "Me and the Guy Upstairs"? What do you think made her develop this attitude?

Answer: Longworth's upbeat attitude is summed up in the advice she gives near the end of the selection: "You can find beauty if you look for it. You got to look for something." Longworth's attitude may have been developed as a stay against adversity; she has found ways to survive many hardships.

◼ *Longworth stayed in a bad marriage until her daughters were grown. How do you feel about her decision? Do you believe that parents who are in a bad marriage should stay together for the sake of their children? Why or why not?*

Answer: Students' answers will vary.

◼ Both Eula Lee Maddox and Louie Anderson stood up to authority figures. What do Alice Lindberg Snyder and Penny Longworth have in common?

Answer: Both are building new lives for themselves as singles. (Other answers are possible.)

5. End the lesson with activities that meet students' needs, interests, and learning goals.

· ·

ACTIVITIES

RHETORIC

First- and Third-Person Storytelling

1. Point out that three of the four readings in the unit are written in the *first person*—with a storyteller who talks directly to readers about an incident in his or her life. "Freedom" is written in the *third person*—with a storyteller who talks to readers about someone else. To illustrate first-person narration, read aloud the first paragraph of "Words in a Blue Notebook." Illustrate third-person narration by reading aloud the first paragraph of "Freedom."

2. To ensure that students understand the difference between the two points of view, have them cross out all first-person references in "Words in a Blue Notebook" and substitute third-person references in their place; e.g.:

● I *She* was six years old, a dirty, barefoot child patting out make-believe tea cakes from mud in the yard of the sharecropper shack where I *she* lived with my *her* father, my *her* two sisters, and my *her* grandmother.

3. Discuss the effects of each point of view. Students should see that first-person storytelling may create a sense of immediacy and rapport between narrator and reader. In contrast, third-person narration may create a sense of distance.

COMMUNICATION

Decision Making

1. Point out to students that each of the people in the readings had to make a crucial decision or decisions. Divide the class into four groups—one for each reading—and assign each group to analyze the decision making in their selection by answering the following questions:

● What decision(s) did the person make?

● What would have happened if the person had made no decision?

● What were the positive and negative results of the choice the person made?

● What other choices did the person have?

● What positive and negative results might have come from each of these choices?

2. Have each group report to the class as a whole.

WRITING

The following assignments may be done in or out of class. Ⓑ designates an assignment suitable for beginning writers; ◼, intermediate writers; Ⓔ, more experienced writers. (Questions that appear in the student anthology are in regular typeface. Additional questions, which appear only in this teacher's edition, are in italics.)

Ⓑ Reread what Eula Lee Maddox wrote in the front of her blue notebook. Then write a few sentences of your own that define who you are and what you want to become.

◼ Louie Anderson wrote letters to his father, even though he was no longer alive to read them. Write a letter to a friend or loved one who has passed away. Tell this person about some recent event in your life, how you feel about it, and how you think this person would have reacted.

◼ *Describe a major turning point in your life.*

Ⓔ Write a short play about the day Penny Longworth left her husband. Include a conversation between Penny, her husband, and the twenty-one-year-old daughter. Give directions on where the conversation should take place and how each person should say his or her lines.

TRADING PLACES

(PAGES 109-129)

· ·

THEME SUMMARY

Each of the people in the four selections traded his or her place in life for something completely new and different. Dr. John Coleman ("Wednesday, February 28") was a college president when he decided to take a year off and go to work as a laborer. Linen Bliss traded life as part of the Eastern elite for marriage to a Montana rancher. As a teenager, Rose Del Castillo Guilbault ("Hispanic, USA: The Conveyor Belt Ladies") traded her middle-class life to work over the summers with Mexican migrants. While he was in college, Richard Rodriguez ("Workers") spent a summer digging ditches.

· ·

STEP-BY-STEP LESSON PLAN

1. Ask the pre-reading questions:

   • Have you ever wondered what it would be like to trade your present life for a completely different one? Perhaps you've wondered what it would be like to have been born in a different family, in a different part of the country, or in a different part of the world. Or maybe you've just daydreamed about leaving everything behind and starting fresh someplace else. If you've ever had thoughts like these, what caused them? What did you imagine your new life would have that your present life does not?

Help students distinguish between fanciful daydreams and more serious thoughts about a different life.

2. Read the purpose statement aloud to help students set a goal for reading:

   • As you read, think about whether each person successfully made the trade. Ask yourself why the person wanted to trade places and whether you can imagine yourself doing the same.

3. Read aloud the first piece ("Wednesday, February 28"), or have students take turns reading the piece aloud. Then review the purpose statement and assign the other three readings. As an alternative, assign each of the readings to a student or a group of students to present to the rest of the class.

4. To ensure that students understand the pieces, ask them to summarize the main idea of each reading orally or on paper. Then ask the following literal **L**, interpretive **I**, and critical **C** reading questions. (Questions that appear in the student anthology are in regular typeface. Additional questions, which appear only in this teacher's guide, are in italics.)

L *Why was everyone on the job with John Coleman ("Wednesday, February 28") in a hurry to cover up the storm sewer pipes they were installing?*

Answer: The workers wanted to hide the poor joints before the bosses saw them. The bosses wanted to hide the joints before the inspector saw them. The inspector didn't want to see the bad joints because he liked the contractor.

I What is Coleman's attitude toward blue-collar, or "laborer," jobs in "Wednesday, February 28"? Do you think most Americans agree with him? Why do you feel as you do?

Answer: Coleman's admiration of blue-collar workers is summed up in the last paragraph of the reading: "To the extent that anyone . . . feels . . . that he is just a goddamn laborer, we have failed as much as if we cheated him in his pay." Students' opinions will vary regarding whether most Americans agree with Coleman's point of view.

I How does Linen Bliss feel about life on the ranch?

Answer: Bliss loves ranch life and feels that it has been good for her children.

L *What new talents and skills did Bliss discover within herself as a result of living on a ranch?*

Answer: Bliss discovered that she was a strong, inventive person who was capable of handling difficult situations on her own.

I How did Rose Del Castillo Guilbault ("Hispanic, USA: The Conveyor Belt Ladies") feel at first about working with the migrant women? How did she feel by the time she quit work for college? What made her change her mind?

Answer: At first, Guilbault was embarrassed; she worried that working with them would stigmatize her and set her further apart from her Anglo classmates. By the time she quit working to leave for college, she had grown close to the women and was proud to know them. Her attitude changed as a result of working closely with the women.

I How did Richard Rodriguez ("Workers") feel when he talked to the Mexican aliens for his boss? Why did he feel this way?

Answer: Rodriguez felt embarrassed and ill at ease. While he knew that the Mexicans recognized his own Mexican heritage, his Spanish was awkward and he wondered how they felt about his being part of the *gringo* work crew. He wanted to identify with them and take their side, but he knew that he was not one of them.

I Contrast Guilbault's and Rodriguez's experiences working summer jobs. Why do you think they had different experiences in similar situations?

Answer: Guilbault was able to bridge the gap between Mexican and American because she worked side by side with the migrant women and because they were proud of the success she represented. Rodriguez was less successful because he did not work directly with the Mexicans and because they associated him with the white American boss.

I *Linen Bliss and John Coleman traded places within the same culture and heritage. Rose Del Castillo Guilbault and Richard Rodriguez traded places from one culture and heritage to another. Which writer do you think made the greatest adjustment? The most successful? Why?*

Answer: Students' answers will vary.

C *Look again at the language in "Wednesday, February 28" and in "Linen Bliss." Which is written in formal language? Which includes slang? Which style of writing do you prefer? Why?*

Answer: Coleman's language is, on the whole, formal, while Bliss often expresses herself in slang. Students' preferences will vary.

5. End the lesson with activities that meet the students' needs, interests, and learning goals.

ACTIVITIES

RHETORIC

Characterization

1. Divide the class into four groups, assigning each group one of the following people to analyze: John Coleman, Linen Bliss, Rose Del Castillo Guilbault, Richard Rodriguez.

2. Ask each group to make a list of character traits that describe the person.

3. Have each group report to the class as a whole.

COMMUNICATION

Roles People Play in Life

1. Point out to students that everyone plays many roles in life. Have students describe the roles played by each of the people in this unit. Ask:

   • What habits, behaviors, ways of speaking, and ways of thinking did the person drop when he or she traded places? What new ones did he or she add?

2. Work with students, using John Coleman's diary entry to demonstrate. Ask students how they think a college president would act and speak and how they think Coleman changed his behavior to pass for a laborer. (You might ask why Dick, the boss, made the comment to Coleman about not expecting anything from laborers. Would Dick have made that comment to his other laborers? If not, what does this imply about Dick's perception of Coleman?)

WRITING

The following assignments may be done in or out of class. **B** designates an assignment suitable for beginning writers; **I**, intermediate writers; **E**, more experienced writers. (Questions that appear in the student anthology are in regular typeface. Additional questions, which appear only in this teacher's edition, are in italics.)

B If you could trade places for a day with anyone else on earth, who would it be? Why?

I What do you think Linen's family and friends in the East thought when she decided to marry Dave Bliss and live on his ranch in Montana? Imagine you are related to her, and write her a letter.

I *Rose Del Castillo Guilbault says that she hopes she has made the conveyor belt ladies proud. What do you think they said to her on the day she graduated from college? What do you think she said to them? Write a conversation between Rose and one of the ladies.*

E Imagine that you are one of the people in this unit and have been invited to give a brief speech to a class of adult students. Write a short speech explaining why you traded one life for another and what you think you learned.

SHORT LIVES, HARD LIVES

(PAGES 131-149)

· ·

THEME SUMMARY

The selections in this unit represent a variety of perspectives on the violence, fear, and sense of hopelessness that plague many of our cities. Mitch Albom ("A Tragedy Too Easy to Ignore") describes how a shooting on a basketball court left a teenager partially blind and paralyzed. Four sixth-graders write about violence in their neighborhood in "Children's Fears." Anna Quindlen ("To Defray Expenses") protests against the apparent acceptance of violence and death in inner-city neighborhoods. Latoya Hunter's diary entry ("January 9, 1991") records the junior high school student's thoughts and feelings about the murder of a neighborhood store clerk. Gary Soto ("Fear") describes the poverty, loneliness, and desire for love that can lead people to commit acts of violence.

· ·

STEP-BY-STEP LESSON PLAN

1. Ask the pre-reading questions:

   • Do you know—or can you imagine—what it's like to live where violence and death occur almost daily? How does it feel to know that the streets where you walk and playgrounds where you play are dangerous?

   Start a discussion by describing your own fears. Ask students whether they believe that the newspapers and TV have helped create unreasonable fears about violence or conditioned us to believe that it is a normal and inevitable part of American life.

2. Read the purpose statement aloud to help students set a goal for reading.

   • As you read each selection, think about how you would feel if the people were your family, friends, or neighbors. Are there ways for people and neighborhoods to be saved—or to save themselves?

3. Read aloud the first piece ("A Tragedy Too Easy to Ignore"), or have students take turns reading the piece aloud. Then review the purpose statement and assign the other three readings. As an alternative, assign each of the readings to a student or a group of students to present to the rest of the class.

4. To ensure that students understand the pieces, ask them to summarize the main idea of each reading orally or on paper. Then ask the following literal **L**, interpretive **I**, and critical **C** reading questions. (Questions that appear in the student anthology are in regular typeface. Additional questions, which appear only in this teacher's guide, are in italics.)

I How does Mitch Albom, the author of "A Tragedy Too Easy to Ignore," feel about the shooting of Damon Bailes? About Bailes himself?

Answer: Albom feels that the shooting is a senseless tragedy. He reveals his compassion and empathy for Bailes when he says, "This is all our story. . . .We are dying, one bullet at a time."

I What is your reaction to the pieces in "Children's Fears"? Why do you feel as you do?

Answer: Students' answers will vary.

L What acts of violence does Anna Quindlen describe in "To Defray Expenses"?

Answer: Quindlen describes two different incidents: the shooting deaths of two students in a high school hallway and the murder of a college-bound teenager.

I What point is Quindlen trying to make by describing the acts?

Answer: Her point is similar to Albom's—we should not allow ourselves to become inured to violence and should try to "reclaim some of the Lost Boys."

C *Both Quindlen and Albom make the same point— we should try to do something to stop the violence that is destroying many of our neighborhoods. Which writer do you think is more effective? Why?*

Answer: Students' answers will vary. Some students will prefer Albom's concrete approach of describing one incident in detail to Quindlen's more abstract, detached approach of examining causes and effects.

I What is Latoya Hunter's ("January 9, 1991") reaction to the shooting in her neighborhood? What does this reaction tell you about her?

Answer: Hunter's reaction—shock and horror— reveals her to be a compassionate person who has not been exposed to much violence.

▮ As the events he describes were happening, Gary Soto's attitude toward Frankie T. ("Fear") changed. Describe the different feelings Soto had about the bully. How do you think the author feels about Frankie now? How can you tell?

Answer: At first, Soto was frightened and intimidated. Then he felt a little superior after listening to Frankie's pathetic attempts to brag about his family's Thanksgiving and Christmas. Finally, when Mr. Koligian beat Frankie, Soto and the other children felt sorry for the bully and frightened for themselves. As an adult, Soto seems to feel pity for Frankie. By opening his story with a description of what happened to Frankie in later life, he implies that even as a child Frankie was doomed. Soto's last paragraph suggests that others in his class could easily have suffered the same fate as Frankie.

▮ In your opinion, what steps should we take to stop the violence in our neighborhoods?

Answer: Students' answers will vary.

5. End the lesson with activities that meet students' needs, interests, and learning goals.

· ·

ACTIVITIES

RHETORIC

Examining Causes and Effects

1. Point out that the selections in the unit describe both causes (reasons for) and effects (outcomes of) violence. To ensure that students can differentiate between causes and effects, provide a model by asking the following questions:

   - What causes the common cold? (a virus)

   - What are the effects of a cold? (itchy, watery eyes; a runny nose; sneezing; a sore throat)

2. Divide the class into five groups, one for each of the readings in the unit. Ask each group to list causes and effects of violence included in their selection. (Warn students that some selections contain only effects.)

3. Have each group report to the class as a whole. On a chalkboard, list all the causes and effects. Ask students to identify other causes and effects not mentioned in the readings.

COMMUNICATION

Managing Conflict

1. Point out that one way violence can be avoided is to teach people nonviolent ways to resolve conflicts.

2. Have students examine the conflict between Damon Bailes and Tyrone Swint, who said he thought Bailes had once attacked him. Ask the following questions:

   - What responses other than violence were open to Swint?

   - What might have kept Swint from taking advantage of these options?

   - What forces might have made Swint choose to react with violence?

   - What part did the availability of a weapon play in Swint's decision to attack?

3. Discuss ways that people can be taught effective conflict-management techniques. To start, you might ask students whether they believe conflict management should become a regular part of the public-school curriculum.

WRITING

The following assignments may be done in or out of class. **B** designates an assignment suitable for beginning writers; **▮**, intermediate writers; **E**, more experienced writers. (Assignments that appear in the student anthology are in regular typeface. Additional questions, which appear only in this teacher's guide, are in italics.)

B In "Fear," Gary Soto writes about a time in his childhood when he was afraid. Describe a time when someone or something frightened you.

▮ What do you think we should do to stop the violence in our neighborhoods? Write a letter to the editor of your local newspaper telling what you think should be done.

▮ *Have you or someone close to you had an experience with urban violence? Describe what happened and how it affected you.*

E In "To Defray Expenses," Dr. Cohall reports that a few young people escape from even the very worst surroundings and go on to make secure, successful lives for themselves. Describe what you think it takes for them to succeed. Do these people share certain characteristics or skills, or are they just lucky? Explain your reasoning.